The Public Economics of the Environment

The Lindahl Lectures

Tax Reform and the Cost of Capital
Dale W. Jorgenson and Kun-Young Yun (1991)

Public Economics in Action:
The Basic Income/Flat Tax Proposal
A. B. Atkinson (1995)

The Public Economics of the Environment

Agnar Sandmo

UNIVERSITY PRESS

OXFORD
UNIVERSITY PRESS

Great Clarendon Street, Oxford OX2 6DP
Oxford University Press is a department of the University of Oxford.
It furthers the University's objective of excellence in research, scholarship,
and education by publishing worldwide in
Oxford New York
Athens Auckland Bangkok Bogotá Buenos Aires Calcutta
Cape Town Chennai Dar es Salaam Delhi Florence Hong Kong Istanbul
Karachi Kuala Lumpur Madrid Melbourne Mexico City Mumbai
Nairobi Paris São Paulo Singapore Taipei Tokyo Toronto Warsaw
and associated companies in Berlin Ibadan

Oxford is a registered trade mark of Oxford University Press
in the UK and certain other countries

Published in the United States
by Oxford University Press Inc., New York

© Agnar Sandmo, 2000

The moral rights of the author have been asserted

Database right Oxford University Press (maker)

First published 2000

All rights reserved. No part of this publication may be reproduced,
stored in a retrieval system, or transmitted, in any form or by any means,
without the prior permission in writing of Oxford University Press,
or as expressly permitted by law, or under terms agreed with the appropriate
reprographics rights organizations. Enquiries concerning reproduction
outside the scope of the above should be sent to the Rights Department,
Oxford University Press, at the address above

You must not circulate this book in any other binding or cover
and you must impose the same condition on any acquirer

British Library Cataloguing in Publication Data
Data available

Library of Congress Cataloging in Publication Data
Data available
Sandmo, Agnar.
   The public economics of the environment / by Agnar Sandmo.
      p. cm. – (The Lindahl lectures)
   Includes bibliographical references and index.
   1. Environmental policy – Economic aspects. 2. Economic policy – Environmental
aspects. I. Title. II. Series.
   HC79.E5 S258 2000   333.7–dc21   00-024726
ISBN 0–19–829798–X

10 9 8 7 6 5 4 3 2 1

Typeset by Best-set Typesetter Ltd., Hong Kong
Printed in Great Britain
on acid-free paper by
T. J. International Ltd
Padstow, Cornwall

CAL STATE UNIVERSITY HAYWARD LIBRARY

Series Foreword

The Lindahl Lectures on Monetary and Fiscal Policy have been instituted by Uppsala University with support from Nordbanken as a biannual event to honour the memory of Erik Lindahl (1891–1960). Lindahl was a great economist who held a chair in economics at the University between 1942 and 1958. A concise but thorough account of Lindahl's scientific contributions with a selective bibliography has been published by Otto Steiger.[1] A more extensive account, including many valuable biographical details, has been presented by Jan Petersson.[2]

Lindahl's contributions fall mainly within four areas:

1. National income accounting.
2. Public finance.
3. Monetary and macroeconomic theory.
4. Stabilization policy.

National accounts are essential for the design of tax policy and stabilization policies. Lindahl developed a consistent intertemporal framework for the basic concept of income by relating it to capital, the pricing of capital goods, and capital gains and losses. He also devoted much time and effort to initiating the empirical measurement of national income movements over time in Sweden. His extremely meticulous work with social accounting concepts has proved to be of such lasting value that it led Sir John Hicks to call him 'the father of Social Accounting theory'.[3]

In public finance Lindahl greatly advanced Knut Wicksell's benefit approach to taxation. His theoretical model for distributing

---

[1] 'Erik Robert Lindahl,' in John Eatwell, Murray Milgate, and Peter Newman (eds.), *The New Palgrave*, New York, Stockton Press, 1987, Vol. 3: 194–8.

[2] 'Erik Lindahl', in Ragnar Bentzel *et al.* 'Economics at Uppsala University. The Department and its Professors since 1741', *Acta Universitatis Upsaliensis. Studia Oeconomica Upsaliensia*, 23 (1993): 71–92.

[3] John R. Hicks, 'Recollections and Documents,' *Economica*, 40 (157): 2–11.

the costs of public goods through a political analogue to markets for private goods is a standard reference in tax policy. He also did a substantial amount of empirical work, directed towards measuring the total tax burden and analysing the effects of double taxation of saving through company taxation. He participated in an international comparison of the burden of taxation in different countries.

Best remembered and most highly regarded among Lindahl's contributions is his pioneering work in macroeconomics as a leader of the Stockholm School. In fact, the term 'macroeconomics' was first introduced into economic parlance by Lindahl. If Wicksell was the first to formulate the idea of 'disequilibrium dynamics', Lindahl was one of the first, and perhaps the first, to develop this into a general area of research. He devised a novel methodology for economic dynamics and introduced many concepts that have become standard in economics, such as temporary equilibrium and the 'natural rate' of unemployment.

Like all Swedish economists of his time, Lindahl was intensely interested and involved in current economic problems and policies. He directed much of his work at finding solutions to the pressing problems of the interwar years, namely, the stabilization of prices, output, and employment. To the Swedish public, he became best known for his fight against inflation after World War II, as an adviser to the *Riksbank*. According to Lindahl, a stable price level should be the declared aim of an independent Central Bank. This target should be reached by using the bank's control of the term structure of interest rates to influence the market's anticipations of future prices.

As Lindahl realized, monetary policy by itself is not sufficient to deal with unemployment problems during depressions. He proposed to complement monetary policy by compensatory fiscal policy, letting the budget balance vary inversely with the business cycle. As Ragnar Frisch stated in 1947, 'Lindahl . . . was one of the first, if not the first, to bring out the view that the essence of problems of public finance resides in the relations that link public finance to monetary policy, and to emphasize the role of the combined monetary and fiscal policy as tools of promoting full employment on a high level of real income and economic welfare.'

Series Foreword

This describes perfectly why Uppsala University has thought it fitting to commemorate the work of Erik Lindahl by a series of lectures on monetary and fiscal policy.

Bengt-Christer Ysander

Uppsala,
March 1991

Preface

The origin of this book lies in the invitation from the Department of Economics at Uppsala University to deliver the Lindahl Lectures for 1996. I am very grateful to the Department for this invitation, and to my friends in Uppsala for their warm hospitality both during the time of the lectures and during a subsequent visit.

When choosing the topic for a series of lectures like this one, one naturally thinks about the person whose memory is being honoured. Erik Lindahl's fame today rests mainly on his pathbreaking contributions to public economics in which he suggested a theoretical framework for an integrated study of taxes and public expenditure. I think that he would have approved of the notion of the environment as a public good and on the emphasis on taxes as reflecting environmental costs and benefits. Since this concern about what Lindahl would have thought coincided so well with what I really would like to talk about, the choice of topic was an easy one.

My own interest in this field goes back to the early 1970s, when environmental pollution was the subject of a lively political debate. I soon became convinced—although it was far from universally accepted—that economic analysis could make some important contributions to the design of environmental policy, and that this in particular was true with respect to what was then known as 'the new public economics'. Since that time, environmental economics has developed into a large area of specialization, while—particularly during the past decade—the environmental dimension in public economics has received increasing attention. This seemed, therefore, a good time to take stock of some of the developments in the field, although I should emphasize that the book does not attempt to provide a complete coverage of the whole literature. My ambition has rather been to provide a survey of what I regard as the more important *problems*, and this has led me to be more selective in my references than would have been the case in a more regular survey of the literature.

The format of the Lindahl Lectures is such that the first of the three lectures should be a general survey of the field which is accessible to a broad audience. This format is reflected in Chapter 1, which can be read by anyone who has had an elementary training in economics. The second and third lectures are supposed to be more technical, and Chapters 2–7 represent extended versions of the material that I covered in the original presentation.

I am indebted to a large number of friends and colleagues who have helped me in the course of my work on this book. Some of them have given me detailed comments on earlier chapter drafts, and I am especially grateful to Vidar Christiansen, Avinash Dixit, Lars Håkonsen and Fred Schroyen. Others have helped me to sort out particular points in discussions and seminar presentations; special thanks are due to Kåre Hagen, Michael Hoel, Erkki Koskela, Ronnie Schöb, Jon Strand and Steinar Strøm. Among my contacts in Uppsala I must especially mention Peter Englund, who provided constant encouragement through the long process of completing the book. In addition, I am naturally indebted to many other colleagues and friends with whom I have discussed issues related to the topic of this book. I would have liked to mention them all, but over a period of thirty years in public economics this group has simply become too numerous to make it possible.

Contents

List of Figures   xii

1. Public Policy and the Environment: An Overview   1
2. Public, Private and Environmental Goods   27
3. Alternatives to Taxes   45
4. The Estimation of Benefits   68
5. The Tax Structure and the Environment   90
6. The Double Dividend and the Marginal Cost of Funds   109
7. Some Further Perspectives   130

References   155
Index   161

List of Figures

1.1.	Strategies for travel to work	7
1.2.	Equilibrium and optimum when the SMC exceeds the PMC	9
1.3.	The efficiency gain from a corrective tax when SMC > PMC	10
1.4.	Equilibrium and optimum when the PMB exceeds the SMB	11
1.5.	The efficiency gain from a corrective tax when PMB > SMB	11
1.6.	The interaction between externalities and monopoly as sources of market failure	13
3.1.	Emissions and clean-up costs	48
3.2.	A non-convex clean-up technology	50
3.3.	Welfare losses with *ex ante* tax and quota	54
3.4.	The determination of the optimal amount of reporting	61
6.1.	Labour-market equilibrium with a monopoly union	119
7.1.	The distribution of gains between countries	138
7.2.	The optimum and equilibrium values of the environmental tax	148

1 Public Policy and the Environment: An Overview

1.1. Introduction

One of the more significant shifts of priorities in economic policy during recent years has been the increased attention given to issues of environmental protection. The issues are both local, national and global and concern both the natural and the man-made aspects of the human environment. As regards the natural environment, people are concerned with the air pollution created by the local chemical factory, or—at the national level—by the country's chemical industry as a whole. The decrease in water quality that arises from the use of fertilizers in agriculture may be both a local and a national issue. At the international level there are the problems associated with global warming, or by the changes in the world's climate that may come about through the uncoordinated commercial exploitation of the tropical rain forest.

The human concern with the natural environment stems—at least for most people—from their belief that the deterioration of the environment will reduce the quality of human life. But from this point of view it is not only the natural environment—the quality of the air, water and soil—which is important, but also the quality of the man-made environment itself. Traffic congestion, noise and deteriorating buildings have negative effects on the well-being of those who live in the cities. People's happiness with the society in which they live is partly determined by the visual aspects of that society—the beauty of the countryside and of city architecture.

There was a time when such social concerns were typically referred to as 'non-economic'. This is certainly no longer the case. Even those who believe that there is a fundamental conflict between economic and non-economic values, must implicitly believe that the two are in some sense comparable when they argue that social welfare may be increased by trading off one type of value against the other.

The public and political concern for the environment in its many dimensions has stimulated research in a wide variety of academic disciplines, including economics. As a matter of fact, economists were early starters in this field, since environmental issues had been introduced in the literature at least as early as 1920, and theoretical concepts had been developed to equip the economics profession with many of the tools needed for a systematic analysis of environmental issues. Today, environmental economics is firmly established as a special field with its own journals and research conferences, and there is extensive collaboration with researchers both from the other social sciences and from the natural sciences.

My aim in this book is to provide a perspective on environmental problems from the point of view of public economics. Public economics is mainly concerned with the study of government tax and expenditure policy and with the proper balance between the public and private sectors, between central planning and the market. Central questions that can be asked within the public economics framework include the following: What is the case for government interference in private markets in the presence of environmental problems? What forms should such intervention take? How should tax policy be designed when the activities of private consumers and firms lead to environmental degradation? How is environmental policy related to the classical trade-off between efficiency and equity considerations?

1.2. The Economic System and the Environment

Samuelson's famous introductory textbook of economics (1958: 16) defined the central problems to be solved by the economic system as 'what, how, and for whom'. The task of any economic system, be it a market system or a system of central planning, is to decide what should be produced, by what kind of production methods, and for the benefit of whom. The criteria used to solve these problems will differ between centrally planned systems and market

Public Policy and the Environment 3

economies; the role accorded to consumer preferences was less important in the Soviet type of economy from that of the Western market economies. Nevertheless, the two types of systems had to provide solutions to the same fundamental problems.

Some environmentalists have tended to analyse the degradation of the environment as inescapable consequences of a market system. The argument is that the market economy is driven by profit incentives, and these incentives are such that the environment is treated as something of no value, i.e. as if it were a 'free good' whose price is zero. It is in particular the manufacturing sector (together with transportation) which has been accorded a central place in this line of argument. The picture painted is one where manufacturing establishments pollute the air, the water and the soil, leading to depletion of natural resources and to the extinction of a number of species of animals and plants, i.e. to a reduction of biodiversity.

It would be foolish to deny that this picture is in many ways a realistic one in terms of our historical experience. But some warnings are also in order. One is that we should be careful about the assignment of responsibility for environmental degradation between sectors and agents of the economy. For example, it has been pointed out in a number of studies that agriculture, in the conventional view one of the 'green' sectors of the economy, is one which contributes heavily to pollution in many countries. Another reason for caution lies in the interdependencies in the economy, which makes it a complicated task to trace the effects of changes in the pattern of private consumption on the structure of production. But a more important warning concerns the implications of the diagnosis for the choice between economic systems. Even if it were right that the environmental problems of predominantly market economies could be ascribed to weaknesses of their incentive systems, it does not follow that recourse to a system of central planning would improve the situation; this would evidently depend on the incentives inherent in that system and in general on the quality of the planning process. The downfall of the central planning system in the former Soviet Union and the other countries of Eastern Europe has uncovered that these countries had disastrous records in environmental protection. In principle, a perfectly informed central planner can always mimic the competitive market outcome and possibly even do better, but to assume that the planner possesses all the relevant information is an extremely unrealistic assumption. Moreover, just as we know that the market system often provides agents with incentives that are socially inefficient, so the planning system has its own set of private incentives that may lead planners and bureaucrats to choose socially inefficient solutions. Environmental problems can be caused by market failure, but also by failures of planning.

The point of view of most economists who have studied these problems is that a rational economic policy towards the environment does indeed require central planning. But if a policy of environmental protection is to be carried out at the minimal cost to society, the policy should include the design of incentives such that individual agents are led to behave in their own interests so as to promote the social goals embedded in the plan. This should be the case both for those individuals who are directly engaged in the planning process and for the private individuals and firms whose decisions are crucial for the eventual state of the environment. This can best be achieved in the setting of a mixed economy, where the design of policy can utilize those incentive mechanisms that already exist in the private market sector.

1.3. Policy Design in a Mixed Economy

One of the most frequently cited passages in economics is Adam Smith's famous statement about the invisible hand in a market economy, by which each individual is 'led to promote an end which was no part of his intention', i.e. 'to render the annual revenue of society as great as he can' (Smith, 1776). A number of writers since then have tried to make Smith's idea more precise by providing more rigorous statements about the efficiency properties of a competitive economy. The modern version of the invisible hand hypothesis corresponds to the two main theorems of welfare economics. These establish the connection between, on the one hand, a competitive equilibrium, and, on the other hand, a Pareto optimum. A competitive equilibrium is a system in which consumers maximize utility and firms maximize profit at given prices, and where the prices are such as to lead to equality of supply and demand in all markets. A Pareto optimum is an allocation of resources such that no reallocation can make one consumer better off without making at least one consumer worse off.

The theorems say that (i) a competitive equilibrium is a Pareto optimum, and that (ii) any Pareto optimum can be sustained as a competitive equilibrium.

In such an idealized market system, what would be the scope for economic policy? One task would be redistribution between individuals and families; competitive markets may lead to efficiency, but they are no guarantee of distributional justice. Another set of tasks would be to provide those goods which cannot be provided by the market. Such goods are known as public goods, and their chief characteristic is that once they are provided, no one can be excluded from benefiting from them. Market incentives cannot function efficiently for such goods, and there is accordingly a role for the government in the efficient provision of public goods.

The policy vision that emerges from this analysis of the proper division of responsibilities between the market and the State is the following: the State leaves the market to allocate private goods efficiently, reserving for itself the tasks of redistributing income and providing public goods. This vision contains a valuable and central insight, but it is in many ways oversimplified. I will focus here on the complications that arise from the different kinds of public goods that exist in the economy.

A classic example of public goods is the national defence. The defence provided for one citizen is the same as the defence provided for his neighbour. The allocation of resources for the production of defence services is decided by explicit political decision-making, budget allocations being made for the various items of defence manpower and equipment. But not all public goods are like that. 'Clean air' is an obvious example of a public good in the sense that my enjoyment of it does not reduce your ability to benefit from it. But clean air is subject to degradation through air pollution, and the amount of air pollution is determined by a large number of individual decisions about car travel, heating of houses, the choice of production technology in firms, etc. In this sense, the production of clean air takes place by means of the reduction of individual production or consumption of pollution-generating goods. We have a case where there is private but uncoordinated production of a public good through individual decisions about private goods. This is what in the literature on welfare economics is known as *externalities*. In this case there is no reason to believe that Adam Smith's invisible hand leads to a socially rational outcome.

Faced with this kind of situation, what should the government do? To see this, take a specific example of an externalities problem such as the traffic congestion of a city centre. This is a multidimensional issue, involving both noise, air pollution, time delays and damage to buildings and streets. There are two types of policy measures that can be used. The first type involves more public spending on infrastructure, such as the construction of roads, tunnels and bridges, providing more parking space, etc. The other type of measure involves the creation of new incentives to encourage behaviour that leads to less congestion. Such incentives could take the form of regulations, such as closing some streets to car traffic, prohibiting parking in certain areas, requiring new cars to be fitted with catalytic converters, etc. They could also take the form of price incentives, e.g. taxing petrol according to its lead content or charging for parking in the city streets. Such measures, designed for the purpose of improving the environment, would also involve costs, either to the public sector in the form of increased expenditure, or to private individuals who would find that they would have to bear a cost either in terms of money or in terms of time use and convenience.

Why would the public sector have to help people to change their behaviour in a direction which is, after all, for their own good? The answer to this problem lies in the public-good nature of environmental externalities. Because each driver's contribution to the level of congestion in the city is so small, he tends to take the level of congestion as given when making his own decision about car use. Seen from his private point of view, he is right. But if everybody thinks in the same way, the result is heavy congestion—a result deplored by everybody. In game-theoretic terms, this kind of situation may be described as an example of the game known as the prisoners' dilemma. Let us suppose that Mr Smith is deciding whether to use his car to go to work (C), or to take the bus (B). The outcome of his decision depends on what the other travellers decide to do. If Smith decides to go by car, he incurs a heavy cost in terms of time, petrol and pollution if all others also decide to go by car; however, his cost will be low if the others decide to go by bus. Correspondingly, he incurs a relatively low cost if he decides to go by bus, provided that the others do the same, but if they go by car, it is very costly for him to go by bus.

Public Policy and the Environment

		The others	
		B	C
Smith	B	(10,10)	(25,20)
	C	(5,10)	(20,20)

Fig. 1.1. Strategies for travel to work

This is illustrated in Figure 1.1, which, for each alternative strategy by Smith and the others, shows the resulting costs for them (Mr Smith's cost being the first term in the parenthesis). The striking aspect of the table is the insight that strategy C is the individually rational choice for Smith, *no matter what the others do*. If he takes his car, he is better off than he would have been on the bus, given that the others choose to go by bus; going by car is quicker, and the petrol consumption costs less than the bus ticket. He is also better off than he would be on the bus if everybody else goes by car, for traffic moves just as slowly as it would have done, had he instead gone by bus. Thus, Smith chooses strategy C.

When we look at the figure, it appears that the rational choice for the others is to choose strategy B, but this presumes that they act in a coordinated manner. If 'the others' constitute a large group of people, each of whom acts on his own, then each of them finds himself in a situation exactly similar to that of Smith, and like him will choose strategy C. The equilibrium of the game is therefore one in which everyone chooses C and incurs a cost of 20. If instead they had chosen strategy B, their costs had been only half as much, but their individual incentives prevent them from achieving this outcome.

The incentives in this game lead to an outcome which is individually rational, in the sense that neither Smith nor any other individual has any private incentive to change his strategy, but it is not socially rational: if everyone could be induced to choose strategy B, all would be better off. In other words, we would have achieved a Pareto improvement. The task of public policy in this type of game is to change the individual incentive structure so as to lead all travellers to choose strategy B.

This picture is of course very much simplified, and especially in that it assumes that everyone is identical. In Figure 1.1, the socially efficient outcome could be achieved by simply forbidding people to travel by private car, thereby forcing them to choose public transport. In a society of individuals who differ with respect to their preferences and needs, this type of policy may not be very sensible. Instead, policy should aim at encouraging a sufficient number of individuals to choose public transport, leaving those with particularly strong needs or preferences to travel by car. This requires more subtle incentive systems than outright prohibition. The most obvious incentive system to study is the price mechanism, and to this we now turn.

1.4. Corrective Taxes in Competitive Markets

The problem that arises in the kind of social situation exemplified by traffic congestion is that each individual does not take into account the cost that he is imposing on the rest of society. The reason that he does not do this is that the market does not charge him with this part of the cost of his behaviour. What the government can do here is to improve the functioning of the market by introducing the missing price component in the form of a tax. This idea is usually traced back to the famous book by Pigou (1920) and is accordingly referred to as Pigouvian taxation. We shall illustrate this in a partial equilibrium setting; later on we shall reconsider the problem in a general equilibrium context.

In a competitive market without taxes, consumers equate their marginal benefit (MB) from consuming the commodity in question to the market price. Producers will choose their output levels to make private marginal cost (PMC) equal to price. In equilibrium the price must be such as to make demand equal to supply, which implies that marginal benefit is equal to private marginal cost.

As our first example of an externality we assume that producers impose a cost on society over and above their private cost, such as in the case of industrial air pollution of residential areas. While the supply curve represents private marginal cost, social marginal cost (SMC) will be higher than this, as shown in Figure

Public Policy and the Environment

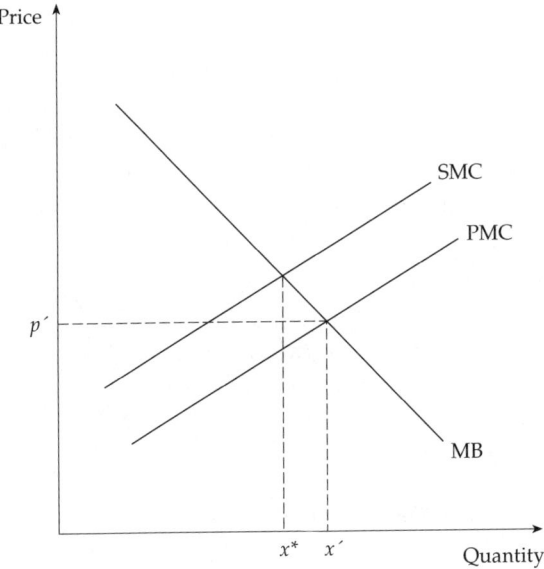

Fig. 1.2. Equilibrium and optimum when the SMC exceeds the PMC

1.2. In a laissez-faire equilibrium, the quantity produced and consumed will be at x' with price p'. However, the socially optimal quantity, which corresponds to the equality of marginal benefit and the *social* marginal cost, is x^*, which is below the competitive equilibrium. Since the market equilibrium differs from the social optimum, there is a case of market failure.

To see how taxes can be used to correct the market failure, consider Figure 1.3. Here the government has imposed a tax on the commodity in the amount of t^* per unit, which equals the difference between SMC and PMC. This means that the consumer price, P^*, is higher than the producer price, p^*, by exactly this amount. At the higher consumer price, consumers have reduced their demand, while the lower producer price has led firms to cut back their output. By using market incentives, the government has led the market to function efficiently; what the invisible hand was not able to do on its own, it has now achieved with the help of enlightened politicians and bureaucrats. The shaded area in Figure 1.3 is the efficiency gain from this policy. The market failure consisted in producing a volume of output beyond that for which SMC = MB. By cutting back that part of production for

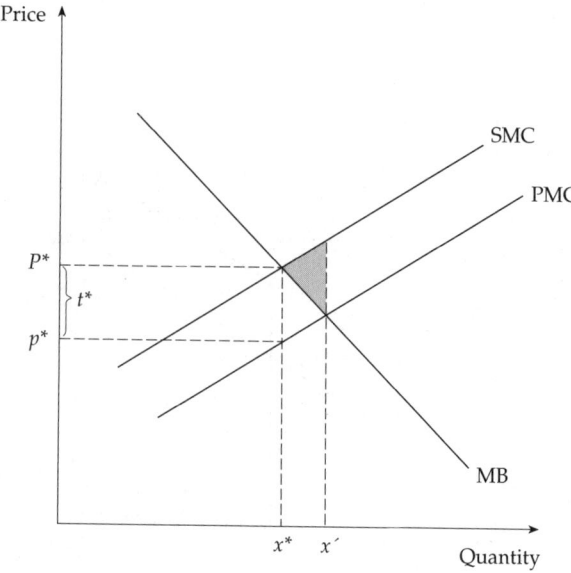

Fig. 1.3. The efficiency gain from a corrective tax when SMC > PMC

which SMC > MB, one has achieved a social gain of exactly this area.

As our second example we take the case where the social marginal benefit of consumption (SMB) is lower than the private marginal benefit (PMB); the traffic congestion example is perhaps most naturally thought of in this way. In this case too the competitive equilibrium involves an output which exceeds the social optimum; the competitive output exceeds the level at which SMB = MC. Efficiency can be restored by a tax which is equal to the excess of PMB over SMB. These points are illustrated in Figures 1.4 and 1.5, which otherwise have a similar interpretation to Figures 1.2 and 1.3.

Some further properties of Pigouvian tax policies should be noted at this point. The first is that taxes do not impose any deadweight loss on the economy, contrary to the usual textbook case. The latter case studies the imposition of taxes in a situation in which the initial market allocation is efficient; in the present case one starts from a situation of market failure, which gets corrected

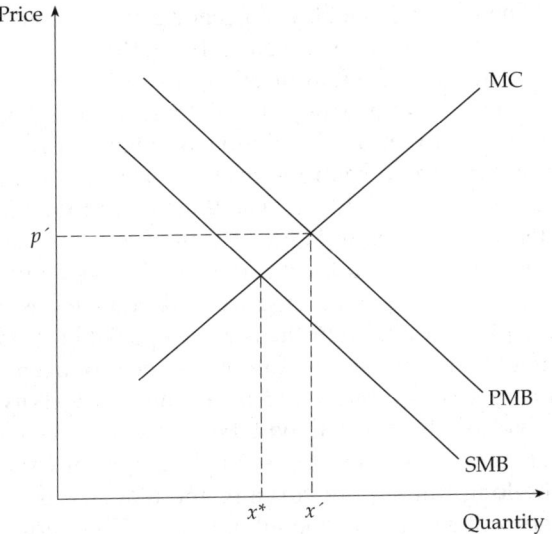

Fig. 1.4. Equilibrium and optimum when the PMB exceeds the SMB

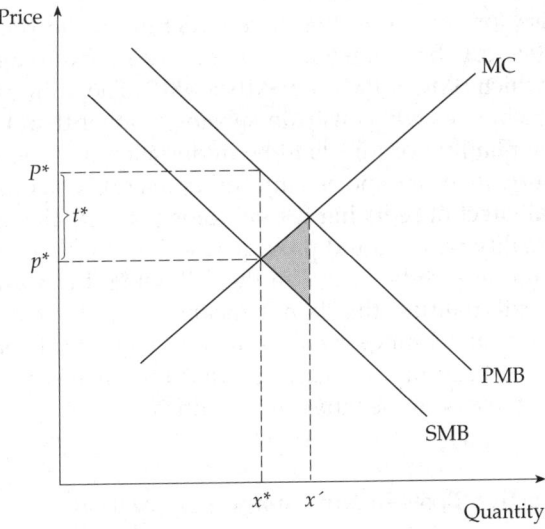

Fig. 1.5. The efficiency gain from a corrective tax when PMB > SMB

by taxes. The second is that the efficiency gain is accompanied by increases in government tax revenue. If e.g. this revenue increase is balanced by the reduction of other, distortionary taxes, there may be an additional increase in social efficiency. It has become common to refer to this as the 'double dividend' of environmental taxation, and there has recently been a lively debate on the precise nature of this dividend. The third point to note is that of the incidence of the tax. In Figure 1.3, the firms impose an additional cost on society, and for this they are charged a price in the form of the tax; this is in accordance with the famous 'polluters pay' principle. But although firms are responsible for collecting and paying the tax, it does not follow that the producers are those who actually bear the burden of it. As the figure shows, a substantial part of the burden will be borne by the consumers through higher consumer prices. In the important special case where the long-run supply curve of the industry is horizontal, consumers will end up paying all of the tax. This shows that the distributional effects of environmental taxes may be less than obvious from purely formal considerations, but it also shows that what matters for efficiency is that the social costs get reflected in prices. Whether the actual polluters pay the tax in a real sense is immaterial from the social efficiency point of view

The case for correcting the price structure in the presence of externalities can be extended to cover *positive* externalities, i.e. cases in which SMC < PMC or SMB > PMB. The optimal corrections in such cases will consist in subsidies rather than taxes. We expect the planting of forests to be undertaken by forest owners for their private economic benefit. But if, in addition, this has the additional effect of reducing the emissions of CO_2, this is a positive externality which could provide justification for a subsidy to the planting of forests. When, in the following, I concentrate on negative externalities, this is not meant to imply that positive externalities are unimportant. But the theoretical principles involved are basically the same, so that little is lost by concentrating on the case of negative externalities.

1.5. Corrective Taxes in Non-competitive Markets

The above analysis was based on the assumption of competitive markets. With non-competitive markets for consumer goods one

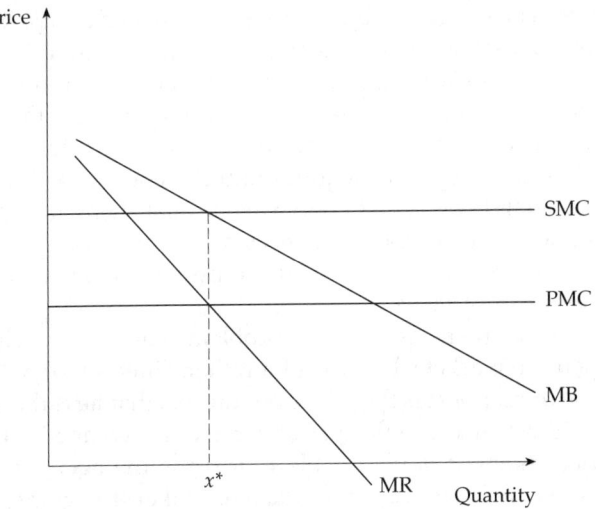

Fig. 1.6. The interaction between externalities and monopoly as sources of market failure

faces the complication that consumer prices are above marginal private cost even without taxes. Is it still a good policy to levy taxes that correspond to the difference between SMC and PMC? Figure 1.6 shows an example of a monopolistic market in which the equilibrium is determined by the equality of marginal revenue (MR) and marginal private cost, which, for simplicity, is assumed to be constant. This leads to a consumer price which is too high, so that this by itself calls for a subsidy, not a tax. However, once the competitive supply has been established, the argument for Pigouvian taxes applies. Thus, the net tax will be the difference between the subsidy and the Pigouvian tax, and Figure 1.6 has been drawn in such a way that the two considerations balance each other perfectly; neither a tax nor a subsidy is required. The interpretation is that the monopoly mark-up is in fact equivalent to the Pigouvian tax, so that the monopolist—by coincidence rather than by intention—acts as the administrator of the optimal environmental tax policy. However, although the efficiency outcome is the same as in the benchmark case, there is a difference in terms of income distribution, since the revenue in this case accrues to the monopolist rather than to the government.

It has been suggested in the literature (Buchanan, 1969) that the monopoly case is in some sense a counter-example to the efficiency of Pigouvian taxes, since the net outcome could be that the polluter should be subsidized to increase output. But the counter-example is only apparent, since the argument for the Pigouvian tax takes the competitive equilibrium as benchmark. Proponents of Pigouvian taxes are of course aware that there are other misallocations in the economy than those due to negative externalities, and corrective taxes and subsidies have in principle to take account of all of those.

However, there is a real problem connected with non-competitive markets, but it is of a rather different kind. Suppose that the monopolist is the single polluter, so that he is the only one who will be subject to this particular tax. In a competitive market of price takers, it is reasonable to assume the agents to be 'tax takers' as well; indeed, this is usually taken for granted in the theory of taxation, whatever the market form is. But the monopolist might not find it rational to adopt a passive behaviour towards the decisions of the political system. Through lobbying and other activities he might in fact try to influence the decisions which are crucial for the magnitude of the tax. If the tax rate finally emerges as the result of a bargaining process between the government and the polluter, the effects of the tax will be harder to predict; it will also be much more complicated to design an optimal tax system.

1.6. The Tax Base

For simplicity of exposition we have so far assumed that the negative externalities can be directly associated with the level of output of the industry in question. This is a simplification. Thus, in the typical real-world case pollution from production activities stems from the use of particular production technologies, sometimes in rather complex ways. If an environmental tax is levied on either output or a particular input, one has defined a tax base which is only imperfectly correlated with the level of emissions, which is of course what we really want to control. In some cases it is possible to monitor emissions, and in those cases the best solution is to have an emission charge. When direct monitoring is not possible, the leading principle should be to design the tax system in such a way as to give producers the right incentives to adjust their decisions in the direction of reduced emissions. If there are possibilities of substitution in production, e.g. between alternative sources of energy, one of which pollutes the environment, then the right incentives are created by levying a tax on the use of the latter source, thus providing an incentive to choose cleaner sources of energy. This tax on an input will normally lead to a higher marginal cost and therefore to a reduction of output. But this is a secondary effect of the proper use of taxes in this case.

The choice of the correct tax base is sometimes a difficult one. The polluting effects of e.g. car use vary with the nature of the roads and streets in which the driving occurs, with the type of car, the time of the day, climatic conditions, etc. In practice it is impossible to design a tax system with rates that vary with all these exogenous variables, and one has to find a tax base which is more roughly correlated with the environmental damage. A tax on petrol, possibly differentiated according to lead content, is an obvious candidate, although it discriminates poorly between different forms of car use. Parking fees that vary over the day or week could be sensible complementary policy tools. In general, there clearly exists a trade-off between the efficiency gains that can be achieved via the fine-tuning of the set of incentives and the costs of administration that increase with the complexity of the tax system.

1.7. Alternatives to Taxes

Taxes are not the only policy instruments which are available for the control of the environment; in practice quantitative regulations are probably much more important. Economists have tended to take a negative view of regulations, since they argue that they tend to result in less efficient social outcomes. Consider the case where a particular form of pollution is generated by the activities of a number of firms, and that a policy decision has been made to reduce pollution to some given level. This can in practice be achieved either by taxing the polluters or by imposing quantitative regulations on them. A central question is now which of these methods is likely to achieve the reduction in pollution at the lowest cost to society. A tax levied on all polluting firms at the same rate will lead to the largest reductions in pollution in those firms where the marginal cost of carrying out the reduction—the marginal cost of abatement—is lowest, and this is obviously efficient. By contrast, regulations will typically have to allocate emission quotas among firms on the basis of some observable historical measure, like output or the input of some particular factor of production, and this will imply that the aggregate reduction of emissions will become unnecessarily costly.

Another solution to this efficiency problem is to make the quotas tradable. If there are many agents in the set of markets governed by this regulatory system, one could envisage a market in quotas that would be at least approximately competitive. Firms with high marginal costs of abatement would then be interested in buying more quota units, while low-cost firms would be interested in selling. This would result in an equilibrium distribution of quotas among firms in which the *average* cost of abatement would be lower, but where the *marginal* cost would be the same in all firms. An equivalent result, at least in terms of efficiency, could be achieved if the government were to organize an auction of quotas, with the total volume of quotas corresponding to the desired reduction of emissions. The distributional implications of the two systems are different, however. Under the first system the firms have the initial property rights in the quotas, and the buying and selling of quotas simply lead to a redistribution of income among firms. Under the second system the revenue from the initial auction of the quotas will instead accrue to the government.

The standard treatment of this set of issues may tend to take a too negative view of quantitative regulations. First of all, there are some types of environmental pollution—such as emitting deadly poison in the drinking water—where the socially optimal level is clearly zero. In such a case it is just as simple to forbid the activity as setting a tax rate which is prohibitively high. Second, compliance is costly to observe. When a regulation is imposed, it is possible for a firm to violate it, sometimes from the consideration that the *expected* fine for non-compliance is less than the cost of compliance. But this obviously means that the expected fine has some of the properties of a tax, the main difference being that the charge for excess emissions is a stochastic one. However, one should also bear in mind that taxes on emissions may be evaded, so that the effective tax rate may also be stochastic. These observations diminish the contrast between regulations and taxes as instruments of pollution control.

An argument often advanced in support of quotas is that their effects are more predictable. If a set of emission quotas is imposed on the polluters, if the quotas are all fully utilized and if there is perfect compliance, the result in terms of emissions can be perfectly predicted. By contrast, the effects of an emissions tax cannot be predicted as long as costs are not fully known. This argument is obviously correct. Note, however, that if the costs are uncertain from the point of view of the policy-maker, there remains an uncertainty about the social costs of meeting the quota requirements. By contrast, if a tax is imposed one may be uncertain about the effects on the level of emissions, but one can be more confident about the cost of the reductions that are actually achieved. First, because the marginal costs of reducing emissions are equalized among firms, the total cost is also the minimum cost of achieving the actual reduction of emissions. Second, if the marginal costs of reducing emissions are increasing, the tax revenue collected will provide an upper limit for the estimation of the total social cost involved; roughly, this is explained by the observation that the tax rate will be equated to the marginal cost, and if this is higher than the average cost, the result follows.

A provisional conclusion is that in the choice between taxes and quotas as instruments of pollution control, one should be sensitive to the nature of the uncertainties involved. I will come back to a more detailed discussion of this issue in Chapter 3.

1.8. Evaluating Costs and Benefits

The discussion so far has avoided the problem of the assessment of marginal social costs and benefits. But this issue cannot be avoided if we wish to know not only if there is a case for a Pigouvian tax or not, but also what its level should be.

We have drawn a distinction between two cases of negative external effects: that in which MSC > MPC and that in which MSB < MPB. It is sometimes a matter of convenience and taste how we classify concrete cases. Industrial air pollution of residential areas may in a number of cases be thought of as reducing aesthetic values—the clarity of vision, the recreational quality of the forest, etc. Although these values may be difficult to assess, what we should like to measure are clearly the benefits as perceived by the individuals themselves, and it is natural therefore to classify environmental pollution as reduced benefits from material consumption. However, in other cases pollution imposes objectively measurable costs on other firms and consumers. Pigou (1920; 1932: 185) refers to an investigation carried out by the Manchester Air Pollution Advisory Board in 1918, which, by comparing the average expenditure on washing in samples of working-class families in Manchester and Harrogate, found that the cost of factory smoke in Manchester was £290,000 per year. An estimate of the Pigouvian tax on smoke emission in this case could be the increased expenditure on washing caused by an additional unit of smoke. Naturally, this would be a low estimate, since no account is taken of other detrimental effects of the smoke, such as the effects on aesthetic values or health. This line of reasoning can take us some of the way towards the computation of the optimal tax, although there will remain elements of consumer benefits that will be hard to capture by means of empirical methods. Still, economic theory can make a valuable contribution to clear thinking about the policy issues simply by working out a theory to guide our thinking in this area. I will return to this in more detail below.

A particular aspect of the evaluation of benefits and costs of environmental pollution arises in an intertemporal context. Protecting the environment typically involves a substantial cost in the present which must be set against benefits that will be reaped far into the future. Environmental protection therefore becomes an investment project, where present costs must be compared to future benefits. The framework of analysis which provides the correct evaluation of such projects is generally accepted to be the present value of the project, computed at some positive interest rate, which, for public sector projects, is referred to as the social rate of discount. Projects are socially profitable if and only if the present value is positive. An implication of such a procedure is that benefits which occur many years from now, will count little for the selection of profitable projects. For example, at a 7 per cent social rate of discount, which is the standard adopted by the Norwegian government, the present value of a stream of environmental benefits of one million kroner per year (estimated at this year's prices), extending indefinitely into the future, would only

Public Policy and the Environment

be about 14 million kroner. This benefit would accordingly not justify an investment in the present of 15 million kroner to improve the environment. Many people would doubtless look upon this as extreme short-sightedness if it is a question of protecting the environment for all future generations.

Clearly, there are two issues here. The first is the choice of a social rate of discount to be applied to all future costs and benefits relative to those of the present, where it is certainly possible to argue that 7 per cent involves an unjustifiable discrimination against future generations. The second is whether environmental costs and benefits should be discounted at a lower rate than whatever is applied to other projects. On the latter issue some would argue that it is difficult to see why one should systematically discriminate in favour of the environmental component of the living standard of future generations. However, against this one may object that if environmental degradation is irreversible, or reversible only at very large costs, there is an additional option value in protecting it which may justify the use of a lower rate of discount for projects of environmental protection.

1.9. Distributional Considerations

In the most stylized version of the welfare economics of externalities, the optimal use of policy instruments to correct market failures can be determined independently of its effects on the distribution of welfare between the consumers in the economy. The reason is that this version assumes that the government can use lump-sum transfers to redistribute income and welfare. When such transfers are possible, commodity and income taxes should never be used for redistributive purposes; in particular, the only use for commodity taxes lies in their ability to correct for the divergence between private and social marginal costs and benefits. But in practice lump-sum taxes cannot be used because governments do not possess the knowledge about the tastes and productivities of individual agents that would be required to implement them. The design of environmental policy therefore has to take account of its distributional effects.

There are two aspects of the distributional implications of environmental policy. First, there are the distributional impacts of the environmental improvement itself. The reduction of traffic in inner city areas will have a different distributional profile from the preservation of unspoilt mountain pastures. Second, there are the effects of the instruments used. For example, the use of commodity taxes on consumption goods (cars, petrol, etc.) will have distributional effects that depend on the income elasticity of the commodity in question. The overall distributional impact of a more ambitious environmental policy has to be evaluated taking both of these aspects into account. Moreover, environmental policy has to be considered in conjunction with society's general policy of redistribution. If progressive taxes and the social security system provide efficient policy instruments for redistribution of income, it is not clear that environmental measures should be designed with a strong emphasis on their distributional effects.

Economists are fond of pointing out that there is a basic trade-off between the goals of efficiency and equality; see e.g. Okun (1975). This is not necessarily true in the area of environmental policy. Suppose that we start from a situation where environmental measures are clearly inadequate, and that Pigouvian taxes are then introduced to improve incentives. There is no particular reason why such efficiency-improving taxes should have an inegalitarian social profile, i.e. they may or may not increase inequality. Whether they do, is evidently an empirical question; the point here is simply that the equity–efficiency conflict is not inescapable. There are parallel arguments in other areas of economic policy. Thus, if a monopoly is forced to decrease its price, this will normally increase overall efficiency in the economy. But at the same time, the redistribution involved in converting monopoly profits to lower prices for the consumers may well contribute to a more equal distribution of the standard of living.

1.10. The International Dimension

Most discussions of environmental policy are set in the context of a single country or jurisdiction. The reasons for this must be sought partly in the structure of specialization in economics, partly by what have been the traditional perceptions of environmental problems in society as a whole. Environmental economics was shaped by research traditions in welfare theory and public economics more than international economics. Moreover, the main issues in environmental policy were seen at least until the early 1980s to be chiefly national or even local.

The main exception to this broad generalization was the concern for the effect of a domestic environmental policy on the country's international competitiveness. Environmental measures, whether they took the form of quantitative regulations or taxes, would raise the costs of domestic firms and make them less competitive both in foreign and domestic markets. While this argument tended to carry great weight in the business community, academic economists were inclined to be critical of it. They would point out that output reductions for polluting firms were an inescapable and indeed desirable effect of environmental policy. Whether these firms became less competitive in comparison with foreign firms or with domestic non-polluting firms would be a matter of indifference, at least in the presence of well-functioning foreign exchange markets. Faced with the possibility that environmental measures could force a domestic firm to close down and move its operations abroad, academic economists would again tend to think of this as an inescapable consequence of a rational policy. If the relocation of the firm were to increase the amount of pollution abroad, that would be a matter for the government of the foreign country to solve.

It was gradually discovered that domestic pollution did not depend on domestic emissions alone, but that many environmental problems were due to emissions in foreign countries, so-called spillover effects. This discovery indicated that environmental problems could not be satisfactorily solved by uncoordinated policies in each individual country, since governments would not have the authority to tax or regulate polluters in foreign countries. International agreements would have to be negotiated by the governments of the various countries involved. The difficulties inherent in this are obvious, since countries' incentives to enter into such agreements would depend crucially on whether they were producers or consumers of pollution. Spillover effects might also change government attitudes towards forcing mobile polluters to move abroad, since they might continue to pollute the domestic environment from their new base, possibly even using a more 'dirty' technology than they did before.

A further step towards a global view of the environmental problem came with the realization that some of the most important recipients of pollution are the 'global commons'—the ocean and the atmosphere. All countries, e.g. by emitting climate gases, contribute to the pollution which may have global warming as one of its effects. This is also a problem that requires coordinated actions by many countries for its solution, but it is also easy to see that there is an incentive problem here that mirrors that which we discussed in Section 1.3 above. Most countries are so small in relation to the global problem that it is individually irrational for them not to take the state of the global environment as given when making decisions that influence their own levels of emissions. This means that each country has an incentive to be a freerider on the policies of others, but if all countries have this attitude, international action will be inadequate.

In spite of the problems arising from the multitude of fiscal jurisdictions, it is clear that there are many insights that can be derived from applying the analytical tools of public economics to international environmental issues. For example, economics has a lot to say both about the desirable efficiency properties of international agreements and the nature of the efficiency–equality trade-off. This will be taken up in more detail in Chapter 7.

1.11. The Political Economy of the Environment

So far we have discussed environmental policy from a normative perspective, considering the choice of optimal policies from the point of view of social welfare maximization. But welfare economics is not a positive theory of the political process; its prescriptions must not be mistaken for forecasts. If we were to provide forecasts of what the future policy in this area is likely to be, the normative theory, in my view, is certainly not irrelevant, since it provides important arguments for the political debate. But we have also to take account of the incentives facing politicians and bureaucrats if we are to gain a deeper understanding of the political process, including those aspects of the process that may lead to policies that are not in accordance with the principles which we have outlined so far.

A natural question to ask is whether political incentives are such as to provide too much or too little of environmental goods. Now it has of course to be kept in mind that, especially when distributional concerns are taken into account, the social optimum is not a uniquely defined allocation, so that the meaning of 'too much' or 'too little' may be unclear. Let us therefore rephrase the question and ask what kind of environmental goods are likely to be especially favoured by the political process and which are likely to receive relatively low priority by politicians.

All environmental projects involve benefits and costs. In the case of Pigouvian taxes, the people who benefit from the environmental improvement are usually not the same as those who bear the burden of the taxes, and in the case of expenditure on abatement facilities, the producer interests in the project will be of a different kind from those of the firms and consumers who benefit from the effects of the project. There is no obvious general answer to the question of which interests are likely to have the strongest influence on political decision-makers. But anyone who has followed the public debate on environmental problems will have noticed the crucial role played by various pressure groups. To form an effective pressure group is costly. The costs will be less, the fewer and more easily identifiable are the members of the group. The power of the pressure group will increase with its size, although at some stage the marginal benefit in terms of power will probably be decreasing. The group will also be more powerful if its members are concentrated in a particular political constituency, regional or otherwise. Whether the groups representing the costs or the benefits of a particular environmental policy will be the more influential, depends on the costs on each side of organizing an effective and powerful pressure group. Loosely speaking, one would imagine that an environmental problem will receive high political priority if the organizational costs on the side of the beneficiaries are lower and their political importance is higher than is the case for those who are paying the costs. This will be particularly likely where a local benefit is paid for through national finance. Conversely, where a national benefit involves a cost to some well-defined local interest, the political priority of the project will be lower. One might also speculate that projects which involve a heavy cost on the present generations with the benefits spread over all future generations will get less political attention than those that also involve benefits for the people who live now.

Political incentives are important for understanding not only the priorities given to particular environmental problems, but also for understanding which solutions will be chosen. For example, although economists have always tended to recommend taxes instead of regulations, polluting industries have frequently expressed a strong preference for regulations. There may be several reasons for this. One reason could be that industrialists believe that politicians will not be able to resist the temptation to use environmental taxes for the purpose of a general expansion of public expenditure; resisting the introduction of new tax instruments may be a sensible strategy to prevent this. Another reason could be that incumbent firms see that regulations will give them a competitive advantage over new entrants to the industry, in that quotas will be distributed according to the existing size distribution of firms, so-called 'grandfathering' of quotas.

There is no reason why one should have to choose between the positive and normative approaches to the study of economic policy; it cannot reasonably be argued that one of these is right and the other is wrong. Both approaches are concerned with interesting and serious problems. Normative economics which offers advice on the design of policy has a need to be informed about the objectives and incentives that motivate political agents. In the positive approach one needs standards of comparison for the study of efficiency and for the analysis of distributional effects. The positive and normative approaches are complements, not substitutes.

1.12. The Public Economics of the Environment: A Short History of Ideas

The first systematic treatment of externalities as a justification for public policy is in Pigou's *The Economics of Welfare* (1920), although the ideas were already present in his *Wealth and Welfare* (1912), and some of the inspiration clearly came from the earlier work of Marshall, his teacher and predecessor as professor at Cambridge. Pigou discusses a number of instances of the divergence between 'social and private net product', e.g. he mentions as an example of a positive divergence between the two the case of 'resources devoted to the prevention of smoke from factory chimneys', because this smoke in large towns inflicts a heavy uncharged loss on the community, in injury to buildings and vegetables, expenses for washing clothes and cleaning rooms, expenses for the provision of extra artificial light, and in many other ways. (Pigou 1920; 1932: 184)

This quotation obviously describes a case of negative divergence, or, as we would now say, a negative externality. Later on in the same chapter Pigou goes on to suggest the use of taxes to bring social and private net products into line, and he mentions taxes on alcoholic drinks and on petrol as examples of practical use of the principle. A shorter treatment of the problem is given in his later book *A Study in Public Finance* (1928). After having described a number of instances of market 'maladjustments' he says that

it is always possible, on the assumption that no administrative costs are involved, to correct them by imposing appropriate rates of tax on resources employed in uses that tend to be pushed too far and employing the proceeds to provide bounties, at appropriate rates, on uses of the opposite class. There will necessarily exist a certain determinate scheme of taxes and bounties, which, in given conditions, distributional considerations being ignored, would lead to the *optimum* result. (Pigou 1928; 1947: 99)

Pigou goes on to point out that taxes and subsidies need not be set at the optimum levels in order to increase welfare, but also that if they are too far from the optimum levels, they may actually lead to a decrease of welfare. He finally points out that any such scheme will have an effect on the distribution of income, and that these therefore need to be taken into account in the design of policy (1928; 1947: 100).

Although later important contributions to the theory of externalities were made by Meade (1952) and others, the subject did not become a central part of public economics until much later. In Musgrave's famous treatise, Pigouvian taxes are barely mentioned, and then, curiously, in the context of distributional, not efficiency, aspects of budgetary policy (1959: 115). In Johansen's textbook (1965), published a few years later, there is a separate section on externalities which is based on partial equilibrium models, but the tax analysis is rather sketchy and related neither to the wider issues of tax policy nor to environmental concerns.

One important contribution which cast doubt on the importance of externalities for public economics—at least in its more traditional sense—was that of Coase (1960), who stressed the importance of the legal allocation of property rights and liability rules as well as private contracts for the efficient settlement of conflicts arising from external effects. In his view the Pigouvian emphasis on taxes was based on a superficial understanding both of the market and the legal system. The importance of property rights, especially the inefficiences associated with common ownership, was also brought out in the influential contribution by Hardin (1968). However, the majority view among economists seems to be that not all problems related to externalities can be solved by a proper definition of property rights. In any case some property rights must be lodged with the State, and then we are back to the standard concerns of public economics.

The interest in environmental policy and its implications for public economics increased rapidly around 1970. A sign of this was that two prominent economists used environmental externalities as their topics for invited lecture series, Baumol (1971) for the Wicksell Lectures and Meade (1973) for a set of lectures in Geneva. An important part of the development since then has consisted in incorporating environmental externalities into the main body of the literature on public economics. My own earlier work in this area (1975, 1976a) showed how Pigouvian taxes could be integrated into the framework of second-best optimal tax theory and thus be liberated from the restrictive assumption that the rest of the economy—including the tax system—had no other distortions. This unified treatment allows a discussion of Pigouvian taxes as part of the more general problem of tax system design. This also includes the analysis of the double dividend issue which has recently been surveyed by Goulder (1995). An excellent recent survey of a wide range of topics in environmental economics is Cropper and Oates (1992).

The modern developments in the area have definitely changed the perception of the role and importance of environmental issues. Far from neglecting the topic, modern textbooks typically devote separate chapters to the theory of externalities, making extensive use of environmental problems to illustrate general theoretical principles, both in the areas of taxation and cost-benefit analysis. The study of environmental policy has become a central concern of public economics.

2 Public, Private and Environmental Goods

2.1. Welfare Maximization

Models of environmental externalities are of many types, focusing on different aspects of basically the same set of problems. But as argued in Chapter 1, environmental goods can in general be regarded as particular types of public goods. In this chapter I therefore begin by constructing a general model which can be seen as an extension of the Samuelson (1954) welfare analysis of an economy with public goods. The extension consists in allowing for the presence of consumption externalities of the 'atmospheric' type, which is the kind of environmental externality that will occupy the centre stage in what follows. This is not meant to imply that externalities in production are irrelevant for environmental policy; the acid rain falling on the Scandinavian peninsula harms not only individual holidaymakers by the lakes and in the forests, but also the firms which exploit the fish and timber resources. But a consideration of consumer externalities is sufficient to illustrate the major issues at stake; in addition, of course, it is the gains and losses of consumers that in the final instance determine the welfare effects for society as a whole. Thus, even pure externalities in production must at some stage be related to consumer welfare.

I begin by assuming that there are $J + 1$ private goods in the economy. Individual i's consumption of commodity j is written as x_j^i, so that total consumption is

$$\sum_i x_j^i = x_j \qquad (j=0,\ldots,J), \tag{2.1}$$

and this is also equal to aggregate production. I follow conventional notation by interpreting factors of production supplied (e.g. labour) as negative quantities of consumption goods.

For public goods of the Samuelson type aggregate production and consumption is z, and the relationship between individual and aggregate consumption is

$$z^i = z \qquad (i = 0,\ldots,I). \tag{2.2}$$

For simplicity I assume that there is only one public good of this kind in the economy; this is immaterial for the analysis to follow.

The amount of environmental externality is denoted by e. This is to be thought of in terms of emissions or environmental deterioration—pollution, for short—and I assume that it is in the nature of a public good (or 'bad'), in that its physical impact on all consumers is the same, i.e.

$$e^i = e \qquad (i = 0,\ldots,I). \tag{2.3}$$

Again for reasons of simplification I assume that there is only one kind of environmental externality in the economy.

The externality is generated by the consumption of commodity J; this interaction with private goods is the main distinction between environmental and other public goods. I shall assume that the amount of externality depends positively on the sum of individual quantities consumed, and negatively on the resources devoted to abatement, a. We can then write the *environmental damage function* as

$$e = e(x_J, a) \qquad (e_J > 0, e_a < 0). \tag{2.4}$$

The functional relationship which is assumed to exist between consumption and the amount of externality is thus an extremely simple one. That it is the total amount, and not more generally the vector of individual quantities consumed, of commodity J which enters the function is the natural way in which to describe the nature of atmospheric externalities. It implies that two individuals' use of commodity J are perfect substitutes as far as the externality is concerned. If individual i decides to use his car less, this will diminish congestion, but if i + 1 increases his car use by the same amount, congestion will remain the same. Note also that since aggregate consumption will be equal to aggregate production, this assumption allows an alternative interpretation of the externality as being generated by production instead of consumption.

Consumer preferences are defined on their consumption of private goods and on the two public goods, so that we can write

Public, Private and Environmental Goods

$$u^i = u^i(x^i, z^i, e^i) = u^i(x^i, z, e) \quad (i = 1,\ldots, I), \quad (2.5)$$

where x^i is individual i's consumption vector. Utility is increasing in x^i and z and decreasing in e. Finally, there is an aggregate production constraint for the economy, reflecting an assumption of constant returns to scale,

$$F(x_0,\ldots, x_J, z, a) = 0. \quad (2.6)$$

Note that since we have assumed that there are no externalities in production, the production constraint does not depend on e.

This model can now be used to analyse the economy's potential in terms of output, consumption and individual utilities. We shall close it by studying the conditions for social welfare maximization, assuming that social welfare can be evaluated by means of a Bergson–Samuelson social welfare function

$$W = W(u^1,\ldots, u^I). \quad (2.7)$$

To characterize the maximum of (2.7) subject to (2.6), taking account of (2.1)–(2.5), we form the Lagrangian

$$L = W(u^1,\ldots, u^I) - \gamma F(x_0,\ldots, x_J, z, a).$$

After eliminating the multiplier, the maximum conditions can be written as

$$u^i_j / u^i_0 = F_j / F_0 \quad (i = 1,\ldots, I;\ j = 1,\ldots, J-1). \quad (2.8)$$

$$\sum_i (u^i_z / u^i_0) = F_z / F_0. \quad (2.9)$$

$$u^i_j / u^i_0 + \sum_i (u^i_e / u^i_0) e_J = F_J / F_0 \quad (i = 1,\ldots, I). \quad (2.10)$$

$$\sum_i (u^i_e / u^i_0) e_a = F_a / F_0. \quad (2.11)$$

$$W_i u^i_0 = W_h u^h_0 \quad (i, h = 1,\ldots, I). \quad (2.12)$$

Here and elsewhere, subscripts are used to denote partial derivatives. (2.8) says that each individual's marginal rate of substitution (MRS) between a private consumption good without externalities and commodity o (which is used here as the unit of account) should be equal to the corresponding marginal rate of transformation (MRT) in production. (2.9) is the Samuelson condition for optimal public goods supply, requiring the equality between the sum of MRS and the MRT. (2.10) expresses the condition for the optimal supply of a private good which generates an externality; we shall discuss this in more detail later. At this point it may only be noted that the condition combines features of the optimality conditions for pure private and public goods, which is very natural, since commodity J occupies a position in between Samuelson's two 'polar cases'; it is a private good for every consumer, but its use produces a public good or 'bad' for society as a whole. (2.11) is the condition for optimal use of resources on abatement, and its form shows that abatement is—at least indirectly—a public good. Finally, (2.12) requires that the marginal social value of consumption is the same for all individuals; while (2.8)–(2.11) are efficiency conditions, (2.12) is the condition for distributional justice according to the evaluations embodied in the social welfare function. This requires that the marginal social value of consumption be the same for everyone.

Although fairly general, the model could obviously have been extended in a number of directions. We have already noted the extremely simplified treatment of production, which, in particular, rules out any consideration of externalites between firms. Another simplification lies in assuming that there is only one public good and only one type of environmental pollution. This is clearly unrealistic, and the assumptions have been made only to make the model more transparent without making it misleading. Finally, we have assumed that all first-order conditions hold with equality, thus ruling out corner solutions. This is also in principle unsatisfactory, since it is far from obvious that an optimum should be described as an allocation where all individuals consume positive quantities of all commodities; nor is it obvious that all conceivable public goods should be produced in positive amounts. Generalizing the model in this respect is not trivial, but in the present context it does not add much to our understanding of the economics of the problem.

2.2. Equilibrium and Optimality

The set of conditions for a welfare optimum provides a standard for the evaluation of the performance of economic systems. The natural standard of comparison here is the competitive equilibrium. We know that in the absence of externalities, and for any given supply of public goods, it will be true that a competitive

Public, Private and Environmental Goods

equilibrium is a Pareto optimum (the first main theorem of welfare economics), and that any Pareto optimum can be sustained as a competitive equilibrium (the second theorem). A competitive equilibrium is defined as a situation in which consumers maximize utility and firms maximize profits at given prices which are the same for all agents, the prices being such as to lead to equality of demand and supply in all markets.

The assumption that consumers, when they maximize utility, take prices as given does not imply that they do not understand the forces of supply and demand. Rather, it means that they understand that variations in the quantities which they consume are too small to lead to appreciable changes in market demand. Therefore, since prices are determined by market demand and supply, they will be not be responsive to changes in individual quantities. Since the amount of environmental pollution, e, is a function of the total consumption of commodity J, it is equally rational for consumers to take e as given when making their choices regarding their consumption pattern, although they may well understand the nature of the environmental damage function. Utility maximization then implies that

$$u^i_j/u^i_0 = P_j \qquad (i=1,\ldots,I; j=1,\ldots,J), \qquad (2.13)$$

where it has been assumed that commodity o is the *numéraire*, having a price of one.

Profit maximization in firms implies that

$$F_j/F_0 = P_j \qquad (j=1,\ldots,J). \qquad (2.14)$$

Taking (2.13) and (2.14) together and comparing them with the optimality conditions, we see that they are consistent with the efficiency conditions (2.8) for the 'clean' commodities $1, \ldots, J-1$. However, they are not consistent with the optimality condition for the externality-generating or 'dirty' good J. For this commodity, an efficient market equilibrium requires that consumers and producers face different prices. Let us define the consumer price for commodity J as P_J and the producer price as p_J. Utility and profit maximization then imply that

$$u^i_J/u^i_0 = P_J, \quad F_J/F_0 = p_J \qquad (i=1,\ldots,I). \qquad (2.15)$$

Going back to the efficiency condition (2.10), we see that the pair of prices will satisfy the efficiency condition if and only if

$$P_J - p_J = -\sum_i (u_e^i/u_0^i)e_J, \tag{2.16}$$

or, defining the tax as the difference between the consumer and the producer price,

$$t_J = -\sum_i (u_e^i/u_0^i)e_J. \tag{2.17}$$

This is the formula for the optimal Pigouvian tax. The tax is equal to the marginal social damage of an extra unit of consumption, which has two components. There is the physical effect, e_J, which captures the damage caused to the environment by increased consumption of commodity J. Then there is the valuation of that damage; because the damage from pollution has a public-good effect, the value of the marginal social damage equals the sum over all consumers of the marginal willingnesses to pay for reduced pollution. By charging consumers with this tax, the government makes it individually rational for them to take the external effect of their consumption into account, although all of them in fact take the amount of pollution as given.

Note that all consumers—which means all polluters—should pay the same tax. That the tax should be the same sounds like the only practical solution, since otherwise the difference in consumer prices might release arbitrage activities and thus not be a stable equilibrium. But note that the uniformity result emerges directly from the optimization model, and that no use has been made of arbitrage constraints. The reason for the uniformity of the optimal tax is that pollution depends simply on the *sum* of quantities consumed of commodity J and not on its individual components. If the latter were the case, individual tax rates should indeed differ at the optimum, and uniformity would have to be imposed as an additional constraint; see Diamond (1973). However, for most applications of externality theory to environmental problems, the present formulation seems to be the most realistic and relevant one.

From conditions (2.10) and (2.11), writing p_a for the producer price of abatement, we can derive the condition

$$-e_a/p_a = e_J/t_J,$$

which is a condition of environmental cost efficiency: The social marginal cost of reducing pollution should be the same whether it is achieved through the curtailing of consumption or by the construction of abatement facilities.

Public, Private and Environmental Goods

This approach to the study of equilibrium and optimality has its obvious limitations. In deriving the formula for the Pigouvian tax on the assumption that for all other commodities, producer and consumer prices are the same, we have assumed the absence of all other distortionary taxes. This implies either that the revenue generated from the Pigouvian tax is just sufficient to finance the provision of the public good, or that any additional revenue requirement can be raised by means of lump-sum taxes. Both alternatives are clearly unrealistic, and a more appealing set of assumptions about the tax instruments available will be explored later. It is clear that moves towards greater realism involve a considerable cost in terms of complexity. When lump-sum taxes are not available, issues of efficiency cannot be separated from those of redistribution and equality, and when one considers the tax system as a source of net revenue to the public sector, Pigouvian taxes must be analysed jointly with other aspects of the tax system. But for such a more realistic analysis, the benchmark of first-best welfare analysis that we have established here remains an indispensable one.

2.3. Assessing the Benefits

What is brought out by the above analysis, in particular by (2.17), is the nature of the information required for the implementation of Pigouvian taxes as well as for the optimal use of resources on abatement. This information, particularly the valuation part of it, is of the same nature as that required to decide on the optimal supply of public goods. Now in the case of pure public goods it has been realized since it was first discussed by Samuelson that there is a fundamental incentive problem with the revelation of preferences for public goods. In the Samuelson analysis, individuals' incentives to report their willingness to pay for public goods depend on the design of the tax system. The most famous example is that of Lindahl taxation, first formulated by Erik Lindahl (1919), whereby each consumer's marginal contribution will be set *equal to* his reported marginal willingness to pay. In that case everyone has an incentive to understate his preference; this is simply his best response, whatever the responses of the other taxpayers. If the government were to act on the basis of the reported aggregate willingness to pay, it would be led to use too little resources on public goods. However, if there were no connection between each consumer's reported willingness to pay and his share of the tax burden, he would have an incentive to overstate his preference for the public good, and the public sector might be encouraged to spend too much of the taxpayers' money on public goods.

This story carries over directly to the present framework of regarding the environment as a public good. In the case of abatement the connection is a direct one, since abatement enters individual utility functions as a public good via the environmental damage function. But since we have seen that the same type of information is needed to implement the optimal Pigouvian tax, it is clear that the collection of information for this purpose runs into the same incentive problem. If consumers knew that the information collected would be used to decide on the optimal rate of tax on commodity J, there would be a particular bias in that those with a high rate of consumption of commodity J would tend to underreport their true marginal willingness to pay, while those with a low—possibly zero—rate of consumption would tend to overreport. This approach to assessment of benefits is therefore considered by many economists to be an unreliable one, due to the lack of incentive compatibility. In spite of this scepticism, eliciting environmental preferences by direct questioning has been a widely used method in this area.

As already noted, there are also less direct and more practical ways of assessing benefits than asking consumers about their willingness to pay. Other methods proceed through the study of market behaviour; e.g. one could estimate people's willingness to pay for a cleaner environment by studying what they are actually willing to pay for housing in clean versus polluted neighbourhoods. Another example is the one cited by Pigou and discussed in Section 1.8 above. The fact that these more *ad hoc* methods are used—and must be used—in practice, does not imply that the more abstract approach taken here is without interest. In fact, the only way of checking whether a particular practical method is a satisfactory one, is to ask whether it is a good approximation to what we would *ideally* like to measure. And the ideal measure of consumer preferences for environmental improvement is the maximum amount that each of them would be willing to pay and still be as well off as he was before. This measure, aggregated over all consumers, is exactly that contained in (2.17).

The view of the purpose of measurement that underlies the present discussion is that the measurement of aggregate willingness to pay is part of the informational input required to implement an optimal policy. Much of the discussion in the chapters to follow is based on the assumption that such information can be collected. We shall return to some of the methods that can be used in Chapter 4.

2.4. The Time Dimension

The analytical framework developed in this chapter is a static one. However, the static nature of the analysis does not imply that the time dimension must necessarily be neglected. As shown by Arrow (1951) and Debreu (1959), the time dimension can be introduced by an appropriate definition of the commodity concept. Thus, we can define $x^i_{j\tau}$ as individual i's consumption of commodity j in period τ, where τ is a number between 0, which stands for the present period, and the time horizon, which is possibly infinite. Similarly, e_τ is the state of the environment in period τ and a_τ the resources devoted to abatement.

Taking account of the time dimension would not add much of interest to the analysis if the problem of optimal resource allocation were separable over time, in the sense that the solution to the many-period welfare maximization problem could be broken up into a series of one-period problems. One of the conditions that would have to be satisfied for this to be the case is that the current state of the environment must only be affected by the current emission of pollutants. But for many environmental problems this is very far from being the case. Many types of environmental damage have a cumulative effect on the environment. Today's emissions are accumulated in the recipients, and the environmental problems of the future will be a function not of the current flow at that future date, but of the accumulated stock of pollutants after adjustment for natural decay or 'depreciation'. Analytically, we can depict this process by rewriting the environmental damage function as

$$e_\tau = e(x_{J0},\ldots,x_{J\tau}; a_0,\ldots,a_\tau), \tag{2.18}$$

which shows the level of pollution in period τ as being determined by past consumption of commodity J as well as by past levels of abatement.

There is a large literature on the dynamic modelling of environmental problems that I shall not go into here. My main point in this connection is that with the incorporation of the time dimension in the model and the new formulation of the environmental damage function the formula (2.17) for the optimal tax rate in the initial period must be rewritten as

$$t_J = -\sum_{i=1}^{I}\sum_{\tau=0}^{\infty}(u^i_{e\tau}/u^i_{00})(\partial e_\tau/\partial x_{J0}).$$

This formula expresses aggregate marginal willingness to pay in terms of the current consumption of the *numéraire* commodity. But this formulation fails to distinguish clearly between environmental preferences on the one hand and time preferences on the other. This is brought out more clearly when the expression is rewritten as

$$t_J = -\sum_{i=1}^{I}\sum_{\tau=0}^{\infty}(u^i_{e\tau}/u^i_{0\tau})(u^i_{0\tau}/u^i_{00})(\partial e_\tau/\partial x_{J0}). \tag{2.19}$$

Here the subjective valuation part of each individual's marginal willingness to pay has been decomposed into (i) his marginal rate of substitution between the environment and the *numéraire* in period τ and (ii) his marginal rate of substitution between consumption of the *numéraire* at times τ and 0. The latter measure is what is usually referred to as i's *subjective discount factor*, so that (2.19) says that the correct benefit measure is the sum of discounted marginal benefits.

In an economy with well-developed capital markets, discount rates will of course not be wholly subjective. Indeed, in the theoretical benchmark case of perfect capital markets, where everyone can lend and borrow at the same market rates of interest, discount rates will be identical across consumers. Letting δ_τ be the *discount factor* for consumption in period τ, we can rewrite (2.19) as

$$t_J = -\sum_{i=1}^{I}\sum_{\tau=0}^{\infty}(u^i_{e\tau}/u^i_{0\tau})\delta_\tau(\partial e_\tau/\partial x_{J0}). \tag{2.19'}$$

The discount factor can be further decomposed as the product of a series of one-period interest rates, so that

$$\delta_\tau = \prod_{\theta=0}^{\tau}(1+r_\theta)^{-\theta}. \tag{2.20}$$

In general, there is no particular reason to expect the discount factors to be compounded from the same constant interest rate, but if we make this additional steady state assumption, the discount factors can be expressed as

$$\delta_t = (1+r)^{-t}, \tag{2.21}$$

where r is the rate of interest. The conditions characterizing optimal taxation and abatement then become

$$t_{J0} = -\sum_{\tau=0}^{\infty}(1+r)^{-\tau}\sum_{i=1}^{I}(u_{e\tau}^i/u_{0\tau}^i)(\partial e_\tau/\partial x_{J0}). \tag{2.22}$$

$$\sum_{\tau=0}^{\infty}(1+r)^{-\tau}\sum_{i=1}^{I}(u_{e\tau}^i/u_{0\tau}^i)(\partial e_\tau/\partial a_0) = p_{a0}. \tag{2.23}$$

The computation of the optimal Pigouvian tax in the present period thus involves three steps. First one has to assess the marginal physical damage caused by present consumption of commodity J in all future periods. Second one must value the damage in every period by the corresponding social marginal willingness to pay. Once these values have been found, the third step consists in discounting them back to the present by using the relevant rate of interest. The determination of optimal spending on abatement involves the same three steps.

It should be emphasized that this is a direct generalization of the static analysis and not an example of the dynamic modelling of environmental externalities. In explicitly dynamic models (see e.g. Siebert, 1995) we would be interested in the time shape both of the quality of the environment and of the policy variables. What we have achieved here is the more limited goal of making explicit the long-run consequences of present policies, and this can essentially be done by the formal trick of reinterpreting the variables of the timeless version of the model.

But more is involved than formalities. Criticism of the public economics approach to environmental problems has been directed both at the concept of environmental preferences involving periods far ahead in time, and at the principle of discounting.

Before proceeding, a remark is in order concerning the assumption of perfect capital markets. Like all assumptions of this kind, it is obviously a theoretical simplification and should not be interpreted too literally. Still, the assumption that the market functions in such a way as to equalize the discount factors across consumers for *all* periods, requires a comment. For fairly short periods this may be an acceptable simplification, but for very long periods it does stretch the imagination, since few contracts involving a fixed rate of interest exist for more than a few years ahead. The assumption that discount factors are the same for all consumers would then more naturally have to be interpreted as an equality of expectations, and the basis for such an assumption is much less clear. Social discount factors for very long periods had perhaps better be thought of as estimates of averages for the population.

Political decisions involving environmental effects several decades from now are taken by today's politicians. If they wish to base their decisions on consumer preferences, the consumers who live now are the only ones available for consultation, either by direct questioning, by observed market behaviour or through political debates and elections. Can these consumers be trusted to take account of environmental benefits that will materialize only beyond their own lifetimes? In the textbook version of consumer theory, individuals care only about consumption during their own lifetime. However, as argued by Barro (1974), if people care about their children, attaching a positive value to their children's utility, realizing that they in turn will care about their children and so on, then today's consumers may indeed act as if they had an infinite lifetime. In that case they would care about future environmental benefits, even though these benefits would occur long after they themselves were dead. If this type of intergenerational altruism is sufficiently strong, no weight should be attached to the popular argument that the government would be justified in overruling the preferences of present generations in the interests of the future. The welfare of future generations is adequately represented by the altruistic preferences of the generations who live now.

But would the environmental preferences of distant generations, even if known, be given sufficient weight? This is the problem of discounting. If e.g. the rate of interest were 5 per cent, one hundred kroner's worth of benefits to those living fifty years from now, would only be valued at 9 kroner by the present generation. Even if the rate of interest were as low as 1 per cent, the future benefit would only be valued at 60 kroner from the point of view of the present. Discounting future benefits at a constant rate has been seen by many as immoral, e.g. by Frank Ramsey, who referred to this as 'a practice which is ethically indefensible and arises merely from the weakness of the imagination' (1928: 544).

However, many people have failed to be convinced by the ethical argument. Instead, they have pointed out that lack of discounting may lead to paradoxical results in project evaluation. Consider as an example an abatement project that requires the current cost of one million kroner, leading to an annual benefit of 1 krone from now to eternity. Without discounting this is a profitable project, while most people would probably feel that the conclusion goes against common sense. Common sense in this case is supported by discounting; even at the modest interest rate of 1 per cent, the present value of the benefits is only 100 kroner.

Thus, discounting seems to leave us with a puzzle. Without discounting, or with discounting at very low rates of interest, major abatement projects in terms of current resource use, yielding insignificant annual benefits over an infinite future, will be profitable. With discounting at what appear to be reasonable rates, benefits that are distant in time will hardly count in a social cost–benefit evaluation.

However, looking back to (2.21) and (2.22), we should note the obvious point that the present value of distant benefits not only depends on the magnitude of the discount factor, but also on the assumed evaluation of environmental benefits at that time. This observation resolves some of the discounting puzzle. To a large extent, the criticism of discounting seems to be based on the view that environmental problems will become more serious over time, whereas the social cost–benefit analysis which is based on discounting, attaches less weight to them the further away they are in time. But if in fact they become more serious, this must be reflected in an increasing marginal willingness to pay, and this will counteract the effect of discounting. This is an important insight. Consider the case of a pollutant that accumulates in the environment. The state of the environment, which is what people care about, will grow worse with each year's emissions. A tax on this year's emissions will therefore have an effect on the environment over an infinite future, and the benefits will have to be assessed accordingly. Even at a 'normal' social rate of discount, a reduction of one unit of emissions in the future could well come to count for more rather than less than a present reduction, once both the growth in marginal benefits and the effects of discounting have been taken into account.

2.5. Uncertainty

The Danish writer Piet Hein is often quoted as having said that 'it is difficult to make predictions, especially about the future.' If one takes it as axiomatic that the past is given, it is only with respect to the future that prediction is meaningful; hence the paradoxical nature of the statement. However, our *knowledge of the past* is certainly not given, so that it is not a trivial matter to predict our future understanding of the past. Historians are busy making discoveries about the past, and the history of environmental pollution is also being rewritten in the light of new discoveries.

However, although changes in our knowledge of the past may alter our view of the future, it obviously remains true that it is uncertainty about the future which is relevant for problems of decision-making in the present. This uncertainty relates both to preferences and technology; in the following discussion I shall simplify by assuming that it relates only to the properties of the environmental damage function, e. Uncertainty surrounds both the effects of current production and consumption and of abatement on the future state of the environment. The degree of uncertainty reflects the present state of our scientific and technological knowledge, and this can of course be improved through research activities. I shall abstract from research in the formal modelling below, but it deserves to be stressed that an important function of research is to diminish uncertainty and make the future more predictable, and this is not least important in the environmental area.

From a formal theoretical point of view the most satisfactory way in which to introduce uncertainty would be to superimpose it on the intertemporal framework developed in the previous section. This could be done in the spirit of Arrow (1953) and Debreu (1959) by introducing the concept of state-contingent commodities. The idea is to define a commodity not only in terms of its physical properties and the time period in which it is available, but also by the *state* of the economy, a state being 'a description of the world, leaving no relevant aspect undescribed' (Savage, 1954). However, because I am not concerned in this context with establishing models of the greatest possible generality, I will abstract from the time dimension and introduce uncertainty in a simple one-period context, in which decisions concerning the environment have to be made at the beginning of the period with the consequences only becoming known at the end.

The uncertainty about the environmental damage function can be captured in a simple extension of (2.4), viz.

$$e_s = e(x_j, a)\varepsilon_s \quad (s=1,\ldots,S). \tag{2.24}$$

Here ε_s is a stochastic disturbance term, which is assumed to enter the function in a multiplicative fashion. This is a special assumption, which simplifies matters without being misleading.

As regards individual preferences over uncertain outcomes, we begin by assuming that these can be represented by expected utilities and subjective probabilities. Let π_s^i be individual i's probability that state s will occur. His expected utility will then be equal to

$$E^i[u^i] = \sum_{s=1}^{S} \pi_s^i u^i(x^i, z, e_s) \quad (i=1,\ldots,I).$$

In the Arrow–Debreu framework of competitive equilibrium analysis one possible assumption is that individuals can trade in state-contingent commodities, i.e. they can enter into contracts that are conditional on the state of the environment. This could be interpreted as an assumption that consumers and firms can buy 'environmental insurance'. But this is hardly a realistic picture of a market economy. The assumption adopted here is that consumers and firms have to make unconditional decisions about consumption and production, that tax policy must be designed with reference to the kinds of commodities that are traded in existing markets, and that abatement decisions must be taken under the same set of conditions.

Writing the social welfare function with expected utilities as arguments, it turns out that the characterization of optimal Pigouvian taxation and abatement now becomes

$$t_j = -\sum_{i=1}^{I}\{E^i[u_e^i \varepsilon_s]/E^i[u_0^i]\}e_j. \tag{2.25}$$

$$\sum_{i=1}^{I}\{E^i[u_e^i \varepsilon_s]/E^i[u_0^i]\}e_a = p_a. \tag{2.26}$$

These conditions are formally similar to what we have seen before; in fact, almost the whole difference is that we now have ratios of expected marginal utilities where before we had marginal rates of substitution. As before there are two components in the marginal social damage from pollution or gains from abatement, viz. the physical effect and the social valuation of it. The social valuation is the sum of the individual marginal valuations, i.e. of their marginal willingnesses to pay. What this formulation makes explicit is that marginal willingness to pay depends not only on preferences as represented by the utility function u^i, but also on individuals' knowledge and judgement, as represented by the subjective probabilities.

This raises a rather deep problem for cost-benefit analysis of environmental measures. Even if we accept the principle of consumer sovereignty, so that environmental policy is to be based on individual preferences, should we also extend this principle to people's probabilities? Probability assessments reflect information levels, and it is by no means clear that the preferences of the ill-informed should count for as much as those of the well-informed. Many would argue, therefore, that there is a case for adjusting people's marginal willingness to pay by correcting or 'laundering' their probabilities (Sandmo, 1983). However, such a procedure has its unattractive features. People express their preferences for environmental goods partly through observed behaviour, partly through voting in elections or referendums, and partly through their participation in public debate. Would the government be justified in wholly or partly neglecting these manifestations of preferences on the grounds that people are poorly informed? One way of avoiding the issue is to argue that the government's duty is to see to it that voters possess the best possible information. But in the case of scientific and technical information, this is easier said than done. It is not clear that there exists a single right answer to this problem, but my own feeling is that, although overriding the revealed preferences of voters may in certain circumstances be justified, the 'burden of proof'— the obligation to defend its position—in such cases falls on the government.

Public, Private and Environmental Goods

A related problem concerns the definition of the state space. We have assumed that each consumer perceives that there are S states, so the partition of the state space is the same for all. But an important part of the information problem is to know the relevant partition of the state space. To take an example, a decade ago few people had even heard about the ozone layer, much less about it being endangered by the emission of climate gases. Part of the growth of knowledge lies in redefining the state space, and it is in the nature of the case that future partitions of the state space cannot be known in the present. This insight limits the use of the model that we have so far been studying.

Assessing consumer preferences for the environment runs into serious problems which are both conceptual and practical. In particular, imperfect knowledge makes one hesitant both about using a concept of consumers' willingness to pay which may be influenced by ill-founded information as well as expert advice which may suffer from similar shortcomings. We learn about pollution and the environment as our experience accumulates. When costs and benefits of public policies are uncertain, there is usually an option value which is important for the timing of policies that have irreversible effects. This point of view has been developed in the important book by Dixit and Pindyck (1994). In particular, they point out that if environmental damage is irreversible,[1] adopting a policy now rather than waiting has a negative opportunity cost of keeping society's options open. This is neglected in traditional cost-benefit analysis, which in this case is biased against the adoption of environmental policy.[2] However, they also point out that there is another possible bias that may work in the opposite direction. This is when the adoption of a new policy requires heavy irreversible investment in abatement facilities, thereby closing some future options for society. Thus, each case has to be judged on its merits, although it seems likely that the former type of irreversibility is more serious than the latter.

---

[1] Irreversibility may be total or partial. An example of total irreversibility is the eradication of an animal species. The emission of greenhouse gases creates concentrations that decay only very slowly (at the rate of about $\frac{1}{2}\%$ per year), so emissions are partially irreversible.

[2] Taking account of this irreversibility would have the same effect as adjusting the discount rate for environmental projects downward. This could help to dissolve the discounting puzzle discussed above.

2.6. Concluding Remarks

In this chapter we have formalized the view of environmental goods as public goods. The environment is a public good in the same sense that was first emphasized by Samuelson; it is available in equal measure to all consumers. But it differs from the standard case of public goods in being produced as a by-product of individual decisions about consumption and production of private goods. The nature of market forces is such that it tends to supply too much of commodities having negative external effects, and the task of public policy is to try to overcome this market failure. It can do this on the one hand by repairing the damage caused by private decisions, i.e. by devoting public resources to abatement. On the other hand it can try to restrain the forces that cause the damage; a number of policy instruments are available for this, but in the present chapter we have concentrated our attention on taxes.

The focus has been on the nature of market failure and on the informational requirement for the implementation of 'ideal' policies, i.e. policies designed for a world of perfect information and no constraints on the use of policy tools. This implies in particular that issues of distributional justice can be disregarded in the design of environmental policy, since this can be taken care of through lump-sum transfers. The assumption of perfect information, although not necessarily of full certainty, makes the analysis relatively straightforward, but it rules out a number of interesting issues that arise in policy design. Alternative policy instruments, which were briefly discussed in Chapter 1, need to be considered further in the light of the assumptions made about information. Moreover, environmental taxes have to be reconsidered as part of a more realistic overall system where taxation also has as part of its objectives to redistribute incomes.

3 Alternatives to Taxes

3.1. The Choice of Policy Instruments: MBI Versus CAC

The analysis of Chapter 2 focused on taxes as the single type of instrument for preventive action against environmental pollution. One justification for that was obviously that taxation is a particularly interesting policy instrument from the point of view of public economics. But in addition, the analysis of the optimal use of taxes is of interest also in indicating the more general informational problems that arise for the implementation of environmental policy, and an understanding of these problems is clearly important whatever policy instruments are used.

Taxation is an example of a market-based instrument (MBI); it is an instrument whose efficiency properties are derived from the incentives inherent in the market mechanism. Other MBIs include subsidies for private abatement activities, auctioning of pollution rights and transferable quotas. Command-and-control (CAC) instruments, on the other hand, are based on quantitative regulation through the legal system, typically by non-transferable quotas, specification of admissible production technologies, etc. Somewhere in between comes the category of policy by persuasion in which the government urges individual agents to change their behaviour in a direction which involves less harm to the environment.

Economists have traditionally been sceptical to policy by persuasion, hostile to CAC policies and enthusiastic about MBIs. In the case of policy by persuasion the main argument is that appeals to people to act in a way that is directly in conflict with their private interest is a shaky foundation for policy. In the case of CAC instruments, particularly quantitative regulations or quotas, the central objection is that they are likely to yield results that are in conflict with the requirements for social efficiency, i.e. Pareto optimality. The contrast between MBI and CAC policies is only indirectly brought out in the formal models that have been discussed so far, and it therefore requires some further explanation.

With negative external effects the laissez-faire competitive equilibrium in effect represents an underestimate of the social cost of production or an overestimate of the social benefit of consumption; this point was brought out in the diagrammatic analysis of Chapter 1. In the normal case[1] this implies that the level of production and consumption will be too high, and the imposition of a tax serves to reduce it. Now it is clear that such a reduction can also be achieved via other instruments. If e.g. all producers are faced with a quantitative limitation on their output—a quota—it must clearly be possible to set these quotas in such a way that the desired output reduction is achieved. As a matter of pure logic this is indeed obvious, but the economist's criticism of quotas is that they normally achieve any reduction in output at an excessive cost, while taxes and other MBIs minimize the cost of achieving a given reduction of output and pollution.

This point is in fact implicit in the formal model of Chapter 2. While the analysis there focused on the optimal divergence between consumer and producer prices, an important property of the optimum, as characterized in particular by (2.8) and (2.10), was that consumer prices should be uniform across individuals. This implies that the tax on the polluting commodity should be the same for all consumers, whether their level of consumption of commodity J is high or low and quite independent of their elasticity of demand. A consequence of this is that those consumers whose demand is price-elastic, will reduce their consumption substantially with the imposition of the tax, while individuals whose demand is price-inelastic will only reduce their consumption by a marginal amount. But when demand is elastic, it means that the cost to the individual, in terms of subjective satisfaction, of cutting down on his consumption is low; conversely, an inelastic demand means that the cost is high. The tax therefore succeeds in allocating the reduction of total consumption among individuals in such a way that it mimimizes the cost of meeting the output target.

Consider by contrast the alternative policy of quotas. Quotas

---

[1] There are exceptions to this generalization, either due to income effects or to the nature of interaction between agents; see Diamond and Mirrlees (1973) and Sandmo (1980).

have to be individualized; there has to be one for each individual consumer. In principle, the quotas could have been allocated among consumers so as to mimic the results of the tax, but this would have required detailed knowledge of individual demand conditions on the part of the government. If instead the quotas were to be fixed in terms of some easily observable characteristic of the consumers, like a fraction of the present level of consumption, this is unlikely to be efficient, since the marginal willingness to pay for an extra unit of consumption (the marginal rate of substitution between commodity J and the *numéraire*) will normally be different among consumers.

An example may illustrate the practical implications of this point. Car use creates significant problems of congestion in many cities. The use of parking meters is an example of a market-based instrument which rations parking space between car users according to their marginal willingness to pay and for that reason satisfies the efficiency criteria that we have already derived in the theoretical model of Chapter 2. But the gradual introduction of meters has also met with a good deal of resistance; it has e.g. been argued that meters are unfair because parking becomes a privilege for the well-to-do. Alternative suggestions for rationing parking space have included proposals for restricting access to the city centre to cars with odd or even registration numbers on alternating days—a nice example of a command-and-control instrument. If the aim is to reduce city traffic by 50 per cent, this is a regulation that stands a good chance of achieving its purpose, and it does so in a way that is arguably distributionally neutral. However, it achieves this in an obviously inefficient manner. It requires the same reduction in car use by those who are greatly inconvenienced by the regulation as by those to whom it really does not matter. Some of the users in the former group will also be encouraged to acquire a second car with a number plate that allows them to drive every day, another example of an inefficiency created by quantitative regulations.

The main point is illustrated graphically in Figure 3.1. For two polluters, A and B, the level of emissions, e, is measured along the horizontal axis, and the cost of reducing pollution, c, is measured vertically. The amount of pollution in the absence of taxes or regulations, e^0, is initially the same for both polluters, while the cost functions are different. As the functions have been drawn,

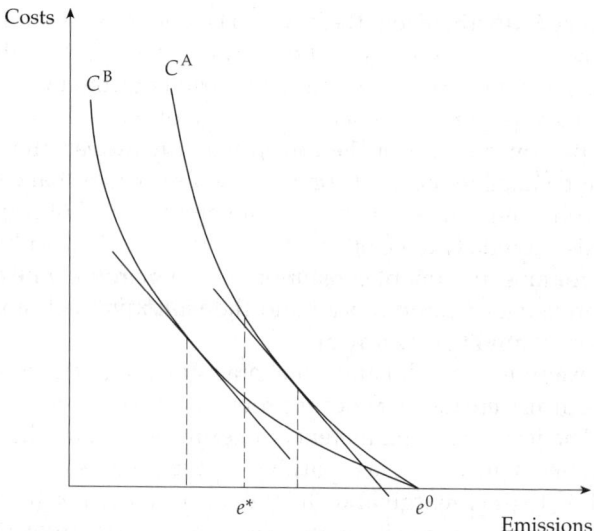

Fig. 3.1. Emissions and clean-up costs

they exhibit the property of increasing marginal cost of pollution reduction. Suppose now that the government wants to reduce the amount of emissions to $2e^*$, i.e. to e^* on average for the two polluters, and that it tries to do so by requiring each agent to emit e^* at the maximum. Now it is clear that in this situation the marginal cost of reducing pollution—the marginal clean-up cost—is higher for agent A than for agent B. Consequently, it would be cheaper for society to allow agent A to pollute more while requiring B to pollute correspondingly less, and this policy should be carried to the point where the marginal clean-up costs are the same. This is shown in the diagram as the pair of points where the tangents to the two cost curves are the same.

The efficient allocation of emissions between the two agents could have been achieved by a tax on emissions. For each unit of reduction in taxes there is now an offsetting cost reduction in the form of lower tax payments. A cost-minimizing agent will then carry the reduction of emissions to the point where the marginal clean-up cost equals the tax rate. And since the tax rate is the same for both, marginal clean-up costs will be equalized, and the efficient solution has been achieved. In Figure 3.1 the optimal tax rate

Alternatives to Taxes

is shown as the common slope of the tangents to the cost curves at the optimum allocation.[2]

A simple formalization of the argument may be useful. Let e^{0i} be the initial level of emissions for firm i, and let e^i be the actual level. The reduction of emissions is then the difference between the two, and abatement costs can be written as

$$C^i = C^i(e^{0i} - e^i) \qquad (i = A, B). \tag{3.1}$$

The functions are assumed to be strictly concave with $C^i(0) = 0$. The government's problem is to find the allocation of emissions which minimizes total costs, i.e. $C^A + C^B$, subject to the requirement that $e^A + e^B = 2e^*$. This is achieved when $C^{A\prime} = C^{B\prime}$.

If the firm has to pay a tax t per unit of emissions, the total cost related to its emissions becomes

$$\varphi^i = C^i(e^{0i} - e^i) + te^i \qquad (i = A, B).$$

Cost minimization clearly implies that

$$C^{i\prime} = t \qquad (i = A, B).$$

and since the tax rate is the same for both firms, the minimization of social abatement costs has been achieved.

This argument seems to provide a strong production efficiency case for the use of taxes instead of quota regulations. It remains a fact, however, that regulations are widely used and, as already indicated in Chapter 1, there are in fact cases where we might expect quotas to perform as well as taxes. These are good reasons for considering them further.

3.2. Arguments for Quotas: Non-Convexities

The argument of the previous section as illustrated by Figure 3.1, was built on the assumption that marginal clean-up costs are increasing. This assumption is certainly plausible, since it seems

---

[2] This approach to the use of Pigouvian taxation does not necessarily imply that taxes are also used to create a wedge between producer and consumer prices. An alternative interpretation of the model is that the government sets an environmental standard in the form of a target rate of emissions and uses taxes or charges to allocate the emissions among the polluters. The standards-and-charges approach was first formalized by Baumol and Oates (1971).

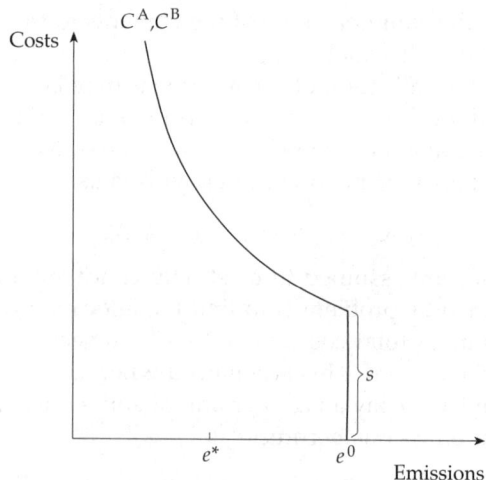

Fig. 3.2. A non-convex clean-up technology

likely that the cost of producing a given increase in the quality of the environment increases with the initial level of quality. It is under the assumption of convexity of the cost function that the argument for MBIs like taxes are particularly strong.

But the plausibility of the convexity assumption is not universal. Suppose e.g. that the abatement of pollution requires some fixed set-up cost, S, for each of the two agents (in this context it is easiest to think of the agents as firms, not consumers). Such costs functions are illustrated in Figure 3.2 for firms A and B. As before, we assume that the government wants to reduce emissions to the level of $2e^*$. For simplicity, the diagram assumes that the two cost functions are exactly alike; the set-up costs, S, are the same for the two firms, and so are the variable costs, C. In this case, in spite of the symmetry between them, it is far from obvious that we would like both firms to reduce their pollution by the same amount. In fact, from a cost-minimization point of view this would only be desirable if

$$2S + 2C(e^0 - e^*) < S + C(e^0 - 2e^*)$$

or

$$S < C(e^0 - 2e^*) - 2C(e^0 - e^*). \qquad (3.2)$$

Alternatives to Taxes

If marginal abatement costs are increasing, the right-hand side of this inequality is positive, so that the conclusion is that both firms should carry out abatement activities if the set-up costs are sufficiently small (as S approaches zero, we get back to the previous case). More generally, requiring abatement from both firms is more likely to be efficient (i) the lower are set-up costs and (ii) the more sharply the average abatement costs (net of set-up costs) are increasing.[3]

Suppose now that the government has carried out this kind of calculation and found that set-up costs are very high, while marginal costs are increasing only slowly. It therefore concludes that the whole of the desired reduction of emissions should be carried out in one of the firms; in this particular case it does not matter which. Should this policy be implemented via taxes or by means of a quota?

In principle it is clear that either method could be used. Having selected one of the firms for the purpose of regulation, the government could either face it with an emissions quota of $2e^*$ or require it to pay a tax that would result in this level of emissions. The other, unregulated firm would not be required to meet any quota requirement or, alternatively, would be tax exempt. But note that one of the arguments in favour of the tax solution has now become irrelevant. In our previous case taxes were efficient because they brought marginal abatement costs into line with each other for all polluters. But in the present case equality of marginal abatement costs is *not* a feature of the efficient allocation; in the regulated firm the marginal cost is $C'(e^0 - 2e^*)$, while in the unregulated one it is $S + C'(0)$. Thus, the tax solution can claim no advantage in terms of efficiency.

Let us now imagine the result of the government's first calculation was different, so that it has found that abatement should be carried out in both firms. This can obviously be done by the use of quotas. It is not quite so obvious that it can be achieved by taxation. When confronted with a tax on emissions, the firm must choose between (i) incurring the set-up costs for abatement and save some tax expenditure from the cutback of emissions and (ii) refrain from abatement altogether and pay taxes on the current

---

[3] This particular example assumes that it is feasible to achieve the emissions target by regulating only one of the firms, i.e. $2e^* < e^0$.

level of admissions. It will choose the former alternative provided that

$$C(e^0 - e^*) + te^* + S < te^0,$$

or, since $t = C'$,

$$-C[1 - (C'/C)(e^0 - e^*)] > S.$$

Since marginal costs are increasing, the left-hand side of the inequality is positive. Thus, if the set-up costs are sufficiently large, the firm might choose the option of continuing emissions at the initial level. The conclusion is that with non-convexities in the abatement cost functions, there is no guarantee that a system of emission taxes will be able to sustain an efficient allocation of emissions between polluters. Non-convexities therefore provide an argument in support of quotas.

This conclusion should not be interpreted as saying that a policy of allocating emission quotas is an easy one to carry out. Non-convexities introduce difficulties for any set of policy instruments that are designed to achieve efficiency. Small changes in technology may lead to large changes in optimal policy. This raises problems for the stability and predictability of economic policy, suggesting that long-run efficiency may sometimes have to be bought at the price of short-run deviations from the efficiency conditions.

The result that non-convexities may imply differential treatment of identical firms raises a tricky problem for the implementation of policy. Clearly, it may be argued that it violates a basic principle of fairness, viz. that identical agents should be treated identically. On the other hand, if the agents in this case are firms, not individuals, one may also ask whether the fairness criterion is at all relevant. After all, social welfare must be derived from the individual welfare of people, not of organizations. However, although the firm as such may not be an agent whose welfare is of much concern to society, there are always individuals whose welfare depends on the fate of particular firms, either as owners or as employees, so that the fairness argument may in fact have to be taken into account as a restriction on a policy of cost minimization. This would obviously imply that fairness is being purchased at the cost of a less efficient allocation of emissions among firms.

3.3. Arguments for Quotas: Uncertainty

As already mentioned in Chapter 1, uncertainty has sometimes been advanced as an argument against taxes and in favour of quotas. It has been stressed that with imperfect information about preferences and costs, the effects of taxes on the amount of pollution may be highly uncertain, while the effects of quotas are alleged to be much more predictable. However, this argument neglects the uncertainty about the costs and benefits involved in the reduction of pollution.

What is the origin of these uncertainties? In part they reflect the limitations of present scientific knowledge. Thus, the emission of a particular gas may have some identifiable effect on human health, but the strength of the effect may be highly uncertain, ranging possibly from the negligible to the fatal. Alternatively, one may simply know that the health effects of this particular gas have never been studied on a scientific basis, so that there may be effects whose present nature are unknown. In other cases knowledge about effects may in principle be perfect, but the effects may depend on some exogenous variable, like the state of the climate, which can only be predicted in a probabilistic sense.

The choice between prices and quantities as control variables in resource allocation problems under uncertainty was discussed in a well-known article by Weitzman (1974). Conceivably, one could account for uncertainty in an Arrow–Debreu fashion by designing a tax on emissions whose rate would be contingent on the exogenous variable in question. But as Weitzman argued, such a tax schedule is a complicated one to design and hard to understand.[4] In most cases of interest, a tax or quota has to be fixed *ex ante*, with uncertainty about the exact nature of costs and benefits.

Weitzman's basic model was one of partial equilibrium with a single producer. The producer's output involves benefits and costs, measured by a concave benefit function and a convex cost function, respectively. Both functions depend on output and on a stochastic state variable. Each of the state variables shifts the functions, so that the precise location of either the cost or benefit

---

[4] But see the critical discussion of this point of view in Ireland (1977), who argues that Weitzman dismisses the possibility of a contingent tax system too easily and presents an example to demonstrate its feasibility.

function is unknown at the time when the policy must be decided. Weitzman's basic question was which of the two control variables that maximizes the expected social surplus (expected benefits minus expected costs). He finds that the issue cannot be settled definitely in favour of either prices or quantities, but that the choice depends on the relative slopes of the benefit and cost functions. A partial equilibrium exposition conveys the spirit of the Weitzman analysis, the point of departure being the benefit-cost figures of Chapter 1.

To fix ideas, let us assume that there is a consumption good which creates social costs in excess of private costs. In terms of Figures 1.2 and 1.3 we have $SMC > PMC$. If we define external marginal costs as $EMC = SMC - PMC$, we can redraw this type of diagram as in Figure 3.3, which shows the Pigouvian tax by the intersection of the benefit function MB and the EMC curve. In the absence of the tax, the MEC would be disregarded by private

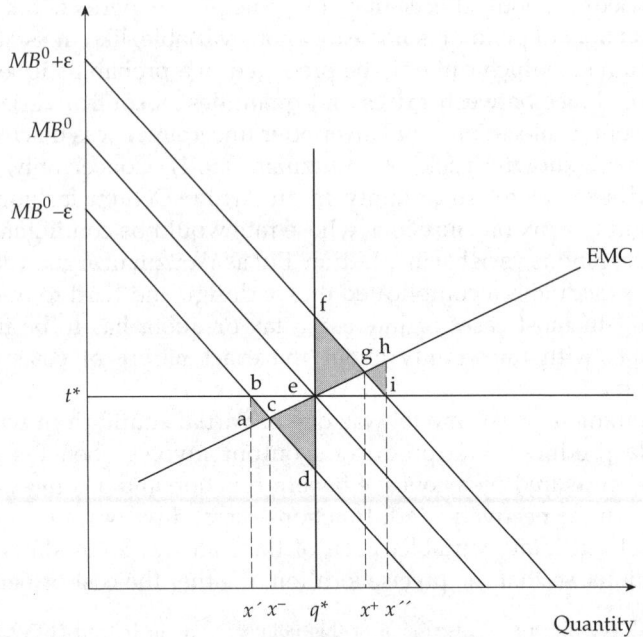

Fig. 3.3. Welfare losses with *ex ante* tax and quota

Alternatives to Taxes

agents, so that the equilibrium would be at the intersection of the *MB* curve with the horizontal axis.

Now assume that there is uncertainty about the private benefits *MB*. To make matters simple, imagine that

$MB = MB^0$ with probability 1/3
$MB = MB^0 + \varepsilon$ with probability 1/3
$MB = MB^0 - \varepsilon$ with probability 1/3

This obviously implies that the expected marginal benefit equals MB^0. A risk-neutral social planner, faced with the problem of maximizing expected consumers' surplus, given linear marginal benefit and cost functions, would then aim to equate *MEC* and MB^0. The intersection of the two curves is at the point *e*.

If the planner chooses to correct for the externality by means of a Pigouvian tax, he will set the tax rate at t^*. How is the result of the policy to be evaluated *ex post*? If $MB = MB^0$, everything is fine; the tax rate is in this case exactly what it would have been, had it been possible to set it after the uncertainty had been resolved. Now look at the case where $MB = MB^0 + \varepsilon$. Consumption will now be equal to x'', which is to the right of the point (denoted by x^+) where *ex post MB* equals *MEC*. The efficiency loss is accordingly the shaded area *ghi*. If instead $MB = MB^0 - \varepsilon$, consumption would have been at x' (instead of ideally at x^-) and the efficiency loss would be the triangle *abc*. The expected efficiency loss is the sum of these two, each weighted by the probability 1/3. Basically, the efficiency loss arises because we have assumed that the tax rate must be set *ex ante* instead of *ex post*.

If, alternatively, the planner decides to use a quota, q^* is the quota which maximizes the expected consumers' surplus. Again, if the expected level of benefits actually materializes, all is well. If the marginal benefits are higher than expected, the efficiency loss is the shaded area *efg*, while if they are lower than expected, it is *cde*. As the diagram has been drawn, it is clear that the tax, although an imperfect policy instrument, is preferable to the quota. It is equally clear that the conclusion is not a general one. To see this, let us rotate the *EMC* curve anti-clockwise around the point *e*. It is easy to see that the shaded areas *abc* and *ghi* then increase in size, while the horizontally shaded triangles diminish. Thus, for a given shape of the benefit function, the tax solution is to be preferred if the *EMC* function is relatively flat, whereas a quota is better if it is steep.

What is the economic intuition behind this result? The first part of the result is easy to explain. Imagine that the *EMC* curve were horizontal. The *ex post* optimal Pigouvian taxes would then have been the same in all three cases, and there is no loss involved in setting it *ex ante* as equal to the expected marginal benefit. Correspondingly, if the *EMC* curve had been vertical, the quantity in any of the three *ex post* optima would have been exactly the same; hence, there is no loss involved in fixing the quantity *ex ante*. If one is close to the former case, the tax solution is best, while if one is close to the latter, the quota solution is the better one. The crossover point between the two occurs where

$$/\text{slope } EMC/ = /\text{slope } MB/,$$

in which the sums of the areas of the two pairs of triangles are the same. Taxes are to be preferred if

$$/\text{slope } EMC/ < /\text{slope } MB/,$$

while quotas perform better if

$$/\text{slope } EMC/ > /\text{slope } MB/.$$

One may also perform the thought experiment of holding the *EMC* curve fixed, while letting the MB^0 curve rotate around point *e*, pulling the two parallel curves with it, the vertical distance between them remaining the same. It can then be seen that the steeper they are, the stronger is the case for taxes, while the case for quotas is stronger if the benefit curves are rather flat. The intuition is basically the same as for the previous case: if the benefit curves are steep, the variance of optimal *ex post* prices is small relative to the expected value, so that little is lost by setting an *ex ante* tax equal to the expected *EMC*. If, on the other hand, benefit curves are relatively flat, the variance of *ex post* prices is high, and the case for quotas is strengthened.

Summing up, if the conditions for the Weitzman model are at least approximately satisfied—linear marginal benefit and cost function, additive uncertainty, the necessity of setting taxes *ex ante*—then taxes should be the preferred instrument for externality regulation if the marginal benefit is more sensitive to changes in quantity than is the external marginal cost, and quotas should

Alternatives to Taxes

be used otherwise. This is a useful insight, although one should be careful with interpreting it as too much of an argument against the use of market-based instruments of environmental policy. It has to be kept in mind that this is the case where taxes or quotas have to be determined in ignorance of either the true costs or the true benefits, and they have to be set independently of the future state of the economy. Neither instrument will in general perform as well as when they could be determined after the true state had become known, and therefore we should not expect an unambiguous ranking of the two instruments to be possible either.

3.4. Taxes vs. Quotas under Imperfect Monitoring

The previous discussion was based on the assumption that a quota, once imposed, is effective in the sense that agents do not cheat by exceeding the quota; moreover, it was also assumed that polluters do pay the statutory Pigouvian tax on whatever the legal tax base is. Both of these assumptions are open to criticism. In the case of quotas, the legal rules governing the quota system will specify a fine for violations of it. The underlying assumption is obviously that agents may try to emit pollutants beyond the quota, hoping that they will not be found out. In the case of taxes, agents may try to evade taxes by underreporting, risking a penalty if they are discovered. This implies that, on the one hand, the fine for quota violations has some of the properties of a tax on emissions, and on the other hand that the effective tax rate may have to be understood in a probabilistic sense. These considerations suggest that the contrast between taxes and quotas may not always be as sharp as often indicated in the literature. Some formalization may help to clarify what the issues are. The following analysis is related to the economics of crime as originally initiated by Becker (1968); more specifically, it takes its basic assumptions from the theory of tax evasion as first formulated in articles by Allingham and Sandmo (1972) and Srinivasan (1973).

Consider a competitive firm which sells a quantity x of a single commodity at price p. Its cost function is $c(x, e)$; this is convex, being increasing in output and decreasing in emissions, e.

Suppose first that the firm is faced with a tax on emissions. It maximizes profit after tax, which is

$$\pi = px - c(x,e) - te$$

with respect to t and e. The first-order conditions can be written as

$$c_x = p \qquad (3.3)$$
$$-c_e = t. \qquad (3.4)$$

These equations determine the optimal amounts of output and emissions (x^*, e^*).

Alternatively, let us assume that the firm is allowed a quota, q, of emissions. Its profits can now be written as $\pi = px - c(x,q)$, and the single first-order condition becomes formally identical to (3.3). However, the solution values are now (x^0, q), and this will coincide with the tax solution only in the special case where $q = e^*$. This special case is frequently referred to as proving the equivalence of taxes and quotas, meaning that it is *possible* to achieve the same combination of output and emissions under the two policy regimes. But recall the economist's standard objections to quotas: if there are many polluting firms, the firms themselves will settle on an overall efficient allocation of emissions provided that they face the same tax rate. With individualized quotas the government will have to set these so as to mimic the tax solution for each individual firm—clearly a very difficult task.

The exposition so far was based on the standard assumption of perfect monitoring of the firm's emissions. Now let us reconsider the tax regime under the assumption that the firm can report a level of emission which differs from the true one. The true level will as before be denoted e, while the reported level is z. The probability that underreporting will be discovered, as perceived by the firm, is α. In that case the firm will have to pay tax on the true level of emissions, and in addition a penalty, θ, which is related to the amount of underreporting, $e - z$. After the firm has made its decisions about output, emissions and reporting there are two possible outcomes in terms of *ex post* profits:

$$\pi^0 = px - c(x,e) - tz \qquad \text{with probability } (1-\alpha),$$
$$\pi^1 = px - c(x,e) - te - \theta(e-z) \qquad \text{with probability } \alpha.$$

I shall assume to begin with that the firm maximizes expected profits $E[\pi] = (1 - \alpha)\pi^0 + \alpha\pi^1$. One consequence of this set of assumptions should be noted right away. If the penalty function is understood as being proportional, with θ being a constant, expected profit is linear in the amount reported. The firm's decision about reporting then depends on the difference between the two tax rates t and $\alpha(t + \theta)$, the latter being the product of the probability of detection and the gross tax rate on excess emissions when detected. If the difference is positive, the firm will not report any emissions, while if it is negative it will report the true amount. In the case of equality between the two rates the firm will be indifferent between reporting and not reporting, and the outcome will be indeterminate.

This knife-edge property of the model is not very satisfactory, and it is natural to look for assumptions that will make the model non-linear, with a solution satisfying $0 < z^* < e^*$ for a range of parameter values. Here there are several possibilities. The one that immediately suggests itself from the standard theory of tax evasion[5] is to introduce expected utility maximization with risk aversion. Another would be to let the probability of detection depend on the reported level of emission. Yet another possibility would be to assume that the firm actually has some concern for the environment, maximizing a utility function which depends both on profit and the level of emission. Finally, one may with some claim to realism assume that the penalty function is progressive in the amount of underreporting. All of these assumptions are of interest and would be worth exploring. I shall begin by studying the last of the four, basically because of its simplicity and realism, to compare taxes and quotas under imperfect monitoring.

In the previous formulation θ is now to be understood as a function of $e - z$ with $\theta(0) = 0$, $\theta' > 0$ and $\theta'' > 0$. The firm's maximand can be written as

$$E[\pi] = (1-\alpha)[px - c(x,e) - tz] + \alpha[px - c(x,e) - te - \theta(e-z)]. \quad (3.5)$$

The first-order conditions for a maximum are

---

[5] See Allingham and Sandmo (1972). Indirect tax evasion has been analysed by Marrelli (1984). An excellent survey is Cowell (1990).

$$c_x = p, \tag{3.6}$$
$$-c_e = \alpha(t+\theta'), \tag{3.7}$$
$$t = \alpha(t+\theta'). \tag{3.8}$$

The firm will set marginal production cost equal to price and the marginal cost of pollution reduction equal to the probability adjusted marginal penalty rate. Moreover, it will carry under-reporting to the point where the probability adjusted marginal penalty rate is equal to the regular tax rate.

A rather remarkable feature of this model, which was first pointed out by Harford (1978), is that the amounts of production and emission will be exactly equal to those predicted by the standard model with perfect monitoring. This is easily seen if we substitute from (3.8) into (3.7); this yields (3.3) and (3.4), and the solution values remain x^* and e^*. If the function v satisfies the condition that

$$\alpha\theta'(0) < (1-\alpha)t < \alpha\theta'(e^*),$$

(3.8) will then imply a positive amount of evasion. But note that the possibility of evasion does not destroy the efficiency property of the Pigouvian tax. As long as all firms face the same tax rate, even if they face different probabilities of detection and different penalty functions, the marginal cost of reducing pollution will be the same for all. The social efficiency property of the standard model therefore carries over to the model with tax evasion.

The economic interpretation of this result is that condition (3.8) is a tax arbitrage condition; the firm will engage in an amount of underreporting of emissions until the point where the expected penalty rate equals the regular tax rate. Rewriting (3.8) as

$$(1-\alpha)t = \alpha\theta'(e^*-z), \tag{3.8'}$$

we may illustrate the determination of z by means of Figure 3.4. The optimal amount of reporting is found at the intersection of the downward-sloping curve showing the expected marginal penalty and the line giving the expected tax if not discovered. Note that if the subjective probability of detection were to differ between firms, and if they also had different perceptions of the penalty function θ, this would have an effect on the amount of reporting, but not on the real amount of pollution, e^*. As the

Alternatives to Taxes

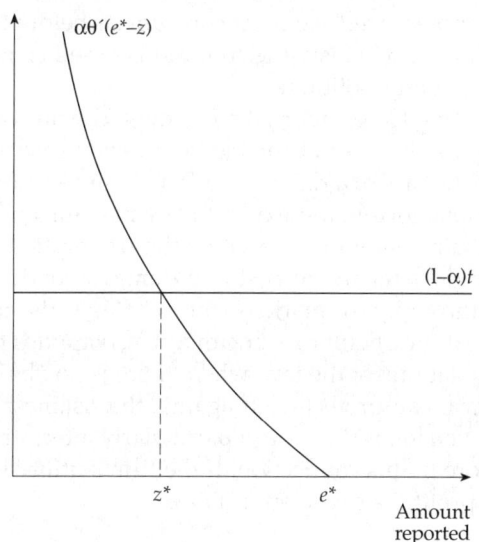

Fig. 3.4. The determination of the optimal amount of reporting

diagram shows, z increases with α and with a positive shift in the marginal penalty function θ'.

Let us now look at the case of a quota. Let the quota be q as before. The firm may decide to emit more than the quota, but it then runs the risk (with probability α) of being detected and fined an amount $\tau(e - q)$. Expected profit is then

$$E[\pi] = (1 - \alpha)[px - c(x, e)] + \alpha[px - c(x, e) - \tau(e - q)].$$

The first-order conditions are now

$$c_x = p, \qquad (3.9)$$

$$-c_e = \alpha \tau'. \qquad (3.10)$$

The crucial question is now whether the allocation of emission reductions will be socially efficient. As shown by (3.10), the firm will equate the marginal cost of pollution reduction to the probability-adjusted marginal penalty rate, which is endogenous. In contrast to the tax case, this rate is not equated to the regular tax rate which is the same for all. Taking account of the fact that cost functions as well as the perceived probabilities of detection may differ among firms, we must conclude as before that a quota system is unlikely to satisfy the conditions for efficient allocation of emissions among polluters.

It is interesting to consider whether these conclusions, particularly the separability result for the tax evasion case, survive the extension to the case of a risk-averse firm. Many economists argue that the proper formulation of a firm's maximization problem under uncertainty should be based on the assumption of risk neutrality, since risks related to cost and demand conditions can be diversified through risk markets. But whatever the force of this argument is, it is difficult to argue that it also applies to decisions involving violations of the law, where there is no obvious way in which the firm can protect itself against the riskiness of its decisions. Risk aversion is therefore a particularly interesting assumption to explore in this connection. If the firm's utility is a concave function of profit, its expected utility is

$$E[U(\pi)] = \alpha U(\pi^0) + (1-\alpha)U(\pi^1), \tag{3.11}$$

and the first-order conditions with respect to x, e and z are

$$(1-\alpha)(p-c_x) + \alpha(1+r)(p-c_x) = 0, \tag{3.12}$$

$$(1-\alpha)(-c_e) + \alpha(1+r)(-c_e - t - \theta') = 0, \tag{3.13}$$

$$(1-\alpha)(-t) + \alpha(1+r)\theta' = 0. \tag{3.14}$$

Here the parameter r is defined as

$$r = [U'(\pi^0) - U'(\pi^1)]/U'(\pi^1), \tag{3.15}$$

and is a measure of the degree of risk aversion. Since the utility function is concave, $r > 0$, and the stronger the degree of concavity, the higher is r.

From (3.12) we have immediately that $p = c_x$, and by combining (3.13) and (3.14) it follows that $-c_e = t$. Thus, the separability between production and emission decisions on the one hand and the reporting or evasion decision on the other carries over to the case of risk aversion. The optimum amount of reporting is determined by (3.14) alone with $e = e^*$. Rewriting (3.14) as

$$(1-\alpha)t = \alpha(1+r)\theta'(e^*-z), \tag{3.14'}$$

we see that the consequences of risk aversion for the reporting decision is to shift the curved penalty function upward, so that

Alternatives to Taxes 63

its intersection with the straight line moves to the right. The implication is that compliance is higher with risk aversion than under risk neutrality.

There is not much point in going into the effects of risk aversion for the case of quotas. Since it has already been shown that a quota system will be inefficient even with risk neutrality, this will a fortiori be the case with risk aversion, when risk attitudes must be expected to vary between firms.[6]

Summing up, the efficiency argument for taxes in preference to quotas has been demonstrated to survive the extension of the analysis to cover tax evasion and quota violations, both with risk-neutral and risk-averse firm behaviour. Imperfect compliance with respect to tax reporting and quota violations does not destroy the basic textbook case for the superiority of taxes.

3.5. Tradable Quotas

Up to this point our analysis has assumed that quotas are initially allocated among polluters according to a principle that does not result in an efficient allocation of emissions among them. This would have required that the quotas be determined in such a way that the marginal cost of reducing emissions had been the same for all polluters, which is exactly the result achieved by the Pigouvian tax solution. In order to implement such an efficient allocation of quotas, the government would have to know the clean-up costs of all polluters, clearly a very demanding informational requirement. With the Pigouvian tax this problem is solved by reliance on the individual information and incentives of the agents. As shown in Figure 3.1, agents with low clean-up costs will reduce their emissions by more than the high-cost polluters, and the reason for this is that high- and low-cost polluters face the same opportunity cost in the form of the tax.

---

[6] The case where firms are required to report their own violations of their quotas offers an interesting further perspective on the properties of quotas. If the firm violates the quota, it risks a fine. But if it underreports the extent of its violations, it risks an additional fine, and this fine is very similar to the penalty rate in the case of tax evasion. It is this similarity which explains the interesting result that self-reporting may lead to efficiency via tax arbitrage. This was first shown by Harford (1987); see also Sandmo (1998*b*) for details.

In an attempt to overcome this inefficiency of quotas, many economists have recommended that quotas be made tradable, so that they can be bought and sold among polluters. Firms with high marginal clean-up costs would then wish to increase their quotas, while those with low costs would be interested in selling off some of theirs. If one could establish a competitive market for such transactions, the result would be a uniform price for quotas, and the marginal clean-up cost would be the same for all producers. Tradable quotas would thus yield social efficiency in terms of the allocation of emissions among agents.

How high would this uniform price be? This question cannot be answered without reference to the supply and demand for quotas, with the supply being given by the politically determined amount of quota units. Suppose, however, that the objective of the government is as illustrated in Figure 3.1, viz. to reduce the amount of emissions from $2e^0$ to $2e^*$, and that it tries to achieve this by allocating a quota of e^* to each firm. This creates an incentive for firm B to sell some of its quota to firm A, and this incentive will persist until the marginal clean-up costs have been brought into line at the quantities indicated in the diagram. But since each of the firms will equate the marginal clean-up cost to the price of a quota unit, this price must necessarily be equal to the Pigouvian tax. Thus, in terms of production efficiency, the tradable quota system is equivalent to that of the Pigouvian tax.

In some other respects, however, the two systems are different. The most important of these is the revenue aspect. In the Pigouvian solution a tax revenue accrues to the government. Under tradable quotas we have to distinguish between two possible regimes. In the first, the government owns the quotas and sells them to firms, e.g. by means of an auction. If one thinks of the quotas as being sold on an annual basis, the revenue from the sale—which could take place through an auction—would necessarily be equal to the annual revenue from the Pigouvian tax. Any sales that were made between firms within the year would simply create offsetting payments and revenues and would thus be irrelevant for this result. If instead the quotas were auctioned off for a longer period, one would expect that the income from this would approximate the present value of the revenue from Pigouvian taxation.

However, this is not the only possibility as regards the allocation of quotas. A second regime would be one where firms are awarded initial rights to certain quotas—so-called grandfathering of quotas—which would then be made tradable. The value of the pollution rights would now accrue to the firms instead of to the government. While the first regime of tradable quotas is equivalent to the Pigouvian tax system both with respect to efficiency and government revenue, the second regime is equivalent only in the first respect, but not in the second.

3.6. Policy by Persuasion: Voluntary Agreements

As indicated above, economists have traditionally taken a sceptical attitude to the idea that problems of environmental pollution can be solved by persuading people to change their behaviour. The standard objection has been that if agents have stable preferences, often alleged to be one of the core assumptions of economic theory,[7] then their behaviour will only change if incentives change. But since environmental quality is in the nature of a public good, the incentive of any one individual to contribute to it is necessarily weak. Little is therefore to be expected from the reliance on individual incentives to protect and improve the environment on a completely voluntary basis. What is required is either governmental coercion (as with non-tradable quotas) or the governmental creation of incentive mechanisms (as in the cases of taxation and tradable quotas).

Among non-economists, however, the use of persuasion as a tool of environmental policy seems to have a wide appeal. One reason for this is probably the reactions of many people towards both taxes and quotas as interference with the economic freedom of agents. The view that agents, if properly informed about the objectives of public policy, will take the necessary action of their own accord has an undeniable appeal to many people's sense of how democracy ideally ought to work.

Is this a too optimistic view of human nature and motivation? There is in fact a considerable amount of casual evidence to

---

[7] The argument for this assumption has been put most forcefully by Stigler and Becker (1977).

support it. People do refrain from littering public places, although—at least according to standard economic theory—they thereby incur a cost while deriving no benefit which can be interpreted according to the view of the environment as a public good. Many people also spend time and money to recirculate old newspapers and return non-refundable bottles. Some also use part of their leisure time to clear up other people's litter, e.g. by joining neighbourhood groups who work to improve the local environment. Others join nationwide environmental organizations to do voluntary work to improve the quality of the environment both in a national and international perspective.

There are obviously two issues here, the first related to the autonomy of preferences and the second to the nature of incentives. As to the first, there is obviously much to be said in general for the assumption of stable preferences from a methodological point of view, but the insistence on it can also be carried too far, and this may be particularly true for problems related to the quality of the environment. A preference ordering is basically a ranking of alternatives, but this ranking depends not only on tastes, but also on information. Many of the most important environmental issues that have been discussed in recent years, like the health hazards that arise from air and water pollution, the consequences of global warming, etc., were quite unknown to most people only a few decades ago. At that time it would have been meaningless to conduct a survey in order to elicit people's preferences over plans to curb CO_2 emissions; with the publicity given to this issue today, this is no longer the case.[8] Preferences therefore depend on information as well as on tastes, and even if one believes that tastes are stable, there is (hopefully) much less of a case for believing in the constancy of information. Through the dissemination of information by the government, the media and voluntary organizations it is therefore likely that the environmental preferences of consumers will change as new information becomes available.

But the incentive problem remains. Even if consumers should realize that global warming is a problem, that does not provide them with an incentive to change from using their private car to

[8] But survey data of this kind still raise difficult problems of interpretation, since some questions implicitly assume a knowledge of the scientific and technical aspects of the problem which many people obviously do not possess.

Alternatives to Taxes

public transportation. Or, to be more accurate, this realization cannot be counted on to change the behaviour of the large majority of consumers.[9] This is the core of the economist's sceptical attitude to the use of persuasion. Unless efforts to create better-informed environmental preferences are coupled with the design of appropriate incentives, there is little reason to believe that environmental policy will be successful.[10]

However, it should be realized that persuasion may take many forms. The government may announce that unless emissions of pollution from a particular industry have been reduced to some specific level by a given date, other measures, e.g. taxes, will be introduced. To the extent that this announcement has an effect on behaviour, it is a weak form of voluntary compliance, since agents in this case simply react to a threat by the government. The threat may well be an effective one, particularly when a small number of polluters is involved. The polluters may decide to act in collusion to reduce emissions in order to prevent the introduction of taxes, and with only a few agents involved a collusive agreement may be relatively easy to negotiate and sustain. But the small numbers assumption is crucial; with a large number of polluters we are back to the previous case with its lack of individual incentives to act for the common good.

---

[9] As pointed out above, many people do behave in a way which can be explained only by their desire to act for the common good. The possibility that the introduction of private economic incentives to solve externality problems may crowd out civic virtues has been discussed by Bruno Frey in a number of papers; see e.g. Frey (1997). For a theoretical model where government intervention leads to less voluntary cooperation see Holländer (1990).

[10] Porter and van der Linde (1995) have argued that environmental regulation of polluting firms might actually increase their profits and competitiveness. According to this view, adopting stricter environmental standards would be in the firms' own interest, and an improved environment would not involve any social costs; in fact, the costs might be negative. This view has been sharply—and in my view convincingly—criticized by Palmer *et al.* (1995).

4 The Estimation of Benefits

4.1. Two Problems in the Estimation of Social Benefits

In the previous chapters we have seen that a number of issues in environmental policy can be discussed without being very precise about the measurement of its benefits. Part of the problem of designing an optimal environmental policy lies in choosing the instruments that are appropriate for the task, and this choice can be settled fairly independently of the amount of environmental improvement that is the target of the policy-makers. But at some stage in the practical design of policy one necessarily has to ask *how high* the Pigouvian tax rate should be or *how strict* regulations one ought to impose. Questions of this kind clearly cannot be answered without a quantitative assessment of the actual size of the benefits, relative to the costs involved. As economists we would like to think of this as taking the form of econometric estimates, but in the majority of actual decisions about policy the assessment is probably much more rough-and-ready. However, even more intuitive methods have to be based on a theory about what kind of indicators of benefits to look for.

Viewing environmental goods as public goods, the model developed in Chapter 2 derived the relevant measure of the social benefit of an improved environment as the sum of individual marginal willingnesses to pay. In the case of an individual consumer the marginal willingness to pay or the marginal benefit is simply his marginal rate of substitution between the environmental good and the *numéraire*; in a market context it is the maximum amount of income that he would be willing to forgo to obtain a given improvement of the environment (or a given reduction of pollution). But unlike willingness to pay for ordinary consumer goods, this willingness to pay cannot in general be expected to be revealed in the market, simply because of the public good nature of the environment. The question therefore arises how one can move from the theoretical concepts to the

The Estimation of Benefits

stage where the theoretical prescriptions can actually be implemented. This involves two steps. The first concerns the estimation of *individual* willingness to pay; one has to find a method for assessing how much an improved environment is worth for a single consumer or producer. The second step is the *aggregation* from individual to social benefits. In the stylized welfare economics model this involved simply the sum of individual benefits, but we have to ask when this procedure is actually justified. Taking the unweighted sum is distributionally neutral, but would not someone with egalitarian sympathies wish to weight the benefits of the poor more heavily than those of the rich?

In this chapter I begin by discussing some of the procedures that have been proposed—and used—for the empirical measurement of individual benefits. I then turn to the aggregation of individual benefits, paying particular attention to the issue of whether aggregation should be 'neutral' or whether account should be taken of the distributional preferences of the government.

4.2. The Revelation Problem

Assuming that the individual consumer knows his own willingness to pay for an improved environment,[1] the obvious approach to the estimation of individual benefits is to ask the question, 'How much would you be willing to pay for an improved environment?' Evidently, the question would have to be related to a more specific environmental problem, but this would in any case be the general nature of the question.

The economist's immediate objection to the question is that there is little reason to expect consumers to answer truthfully. The reason for this attitude goes back to Samuelson's (1954) classic formulation of the theory of public goods. In the context of a discussion of the benefit principle of taxation he pointed out that if individuals believe that their actual payment will be positively related to their stated willingness to pay, they will have an

---

[1] As discussed in Ch. 2, this assumption is not always justified, since people may be poorly informed about the severity of the problem and the likely costs and consequences of policy measures. If that is the case, such a question might not be very meaningful, and the answers would be difficult to interpret. This point is taken up again in Section 4.4.

incentive to underreport their willingness to pay, hoping to freeride on the supply of public goods which is financed by the contributions of others. If, to the contrary, they believe that there is no connection between their stated willingness to pay and the amount of their contribution, they will have an incentive to overstate their benefits or willingness to pay, since a high level of reported benefits might increase the supply of a good that they would get for free, at least on the margin. The theoretical presumption is accordingly that in the case of public goods consumers do not have incentives to reveal their preferences correctly.

How important the revelation problem actually is, has been a matter of some debate in the literature. A famous experiment by Bohm (1972) indicated that the problem might be of less importance in practice than theoretical discussions have tended to suggest. Johansen (1977a) argued than in an open political process there would in fact be strong incentives for elected politicians to vote according to their true preferences, or at least according to the preferences that their electorate believes to be their true ones.

Since environmental goods are public goods, the literature on the estimation of preferences for public goods is of direct relevance for environmental economics, and environmental economists have in fact been prominent in the search for reliable methods of preference estimation. There is an extensive literature in this area which includes both theoretical contributions and a large number of applications that differ both with respect to the nature of pollution and with respect to the area of producer or consumer activity where the environmental problem arises. Here I shall refrain from going into the details of application and instead concentrate on basic principles. For more details and references to the literature the reader is referred to the valuable survey by Cropper and Oates (1992).

4.3. Indirect Methods

In the model of Chapter 2 the consumer's preferences were assumed to depend on the amounts of private goods consumed and on the supply of public goods, including environmental goods. The analysis focused on the derivation of social optimal-

The Estimation of Benefits

ity conditions and did not study the demand-and-supply behaviour of the consumers in any detail; it was simply noted that utility maximization implied the equality (2.13) between marginal rates of substitution and relative prices. It will now be useful to take a second look at the consumer's optimization problem. Since to begin with we are just concerned with the behaviour of a single consumer, we drop the superscript i that was introduced in Chapter 2.

The utility function of the single consumer is

$$u = u(x_0, x_1, \ldots, x_J, z, e), \tag{4.1}$$

and his budget constraint is

$$\Sigma_j P_j x_j = y, \tag{4.2}$$

where y is any lump-sum income that the consumer might receive. Utility maximization now implies the demand functions

$$x_j = x_j(P, y, z, e) \quad (j = 0, 1, \ldots, J), \tag{4.3}$$

where P is the vector of consumer prices, as well as the indirect utility function

$$v = v(P, y, z, e). \tag{4.4}$$

The important point to note is that the demand functions depend not only on prices and income but also on the environment (as well as the supply of public goods). This could be given a very wide interpretation as the whole physical, institutional and social environment, and aspects of this wide interpretation are captured in the dependence of market behaviour on public and environmental goods. Note that if the utility function (4.1) had been written as separable in e, e.g. on the additive form $u = \phi(x_0, x_1, \ldots, x_J, z) + \psi(e)$, then behaviour would have been independent of the environment,[2] although utility would not. In this case then, individuals suffer from environmental degradation, but it does not affect the way they act. Thus, the assumption of separability implies that the demand for recreational goods and services will

---

[2] The point is that with separability the marginal rates of substitution between private goods will be independent of e; since the equalities between these and relative prices, together with the budget constraint, determine the demand functions, the result follows.

be independent of air and water pollution, and traffic congestion will be irrelevant as an explanation of car use. This is plainly unrealistic, and indirect methods of benefit estimation in fact take as their point of departure that the separability assumption is not satisfied and that changes in the environment lead to observable changes in people's market behaviour.

A unifying theoretical framework for indirect methods of benefit estimation can be obtained through application of the household production approach, as originally proposed—using somewhat different formulations—by Becker (1965), Lancaster (1966) and Muth (1966) and developed in the public goods context in Sandmo (1973). Let us assume that utility is defined not directly on commodities, x_j, but on a number of activities or final goods, c_k. The quantity of a final good consumed is produced in the household by means of inputs partly of private goods (one of which might be time), partly of public and environmental goods. For example, individual transportation services could be thought of as being produced in part by private-good inputs like the private car, petrol and the driver's time, in part by produced public goods like roads and public safety devices, and in part by environmental characteristics like congestion. To simplify, let us assume that final good k is produced by means of the single private good j and an environmental good e. The household production function would then be

$$c_k = c_k(x_j, e), \tag{4.5}$$

which we may assume to be increasing in x_j and decreasing in e. We further assume that x_j and e do not enter any other production function for final goods.

Unlike the utility function, this production relationship is assumed to be objectively given and directly observable; experts can observe and estimate what the effect on individual driving time would be of an increase in traffic congestion. Using this framework, how can we derive the consumer's marginal willingness to pay for an improved environment? To illustrate, we assume that there are K final goods but that market commodity 0 enters the utility function directly and can be used as the numéraire.[3] We can then write the utility function as

---

[3] The assumption is that there is one good which is valued for its own sake and not as an input into a household production process. This assumption is made for convenience only.

The Estimation of Benefits

$$u = u(x_0, c_1, \ldots, c_k, \ldots, c_K), \quad (4.6)$$

where (4.5) holds for final good k, and where we do not need to specify exactly how household production of the other final goods depends on private and public inputs. What we are interested in is the marginal rate of substitution between the environmental good and the *numéraire*, which can be computed as

$$u_e/u_0 = u_k(\partial c_k/\partial e)/u_0. \quad (4.7)$$

For any pair of private goods the consumer will equate his marginal rate of substitution to the ratio of prices; since the price of commodity 0 is unity, this implies that

$$u_k(\partial c_k/\partial x_j)/u_0 = P_j. \quad (4.8)$$

Substituting this into (4.7) we obtain

$$u_e/u_0 = P_j(\partial c_k/\partial e)/(\partial c_k/\partial x_j). \quad (4.9)$$

The right-hand side of this equation has now been written as the product of two magnitudes, both of which are independent of any knowledge of individual preferences. The first is the consumer price of market commodity j, while the second is the marginal technical rate of substitution in the household production function between that commodity and the environment. The whole expression has an obvious interpretation as the reduced expenditure on commodity j which follows from a given reduction of environmental pollution, holding the amount of the final good, c_k, constant.

The example mentioned by Pigou (1920), and which was presented in Chapter 1, fits nicely into this framework of analysis. The cleanliness of a household's living conditions can be seen as a final good (c_k) that is valued by the household. A reduction of air pollution (e) increases the available amount of this good, and the household compensates for this by cutting back its expenditure on soap, detergent, etc. (x_j), the consumer price of which is P_j. The example can be regarded as an illustration of what Cropper and Oates (1992) refer to as *averting behaviour*, where increased use of private goods can be used to compensate for the effect of a decline of environmental quality. Another example that they mention is where 'residents of smoggy areas can take medicine to relieve itchy eyes and runny noses' (1992: 703). Applying the same approach to production in firms, an example would be where fishermen purchase chemicals to restore the calcium content of a lake when it has been reduced by acid rain.

The household production approach has, however, a more general applicability to environmental problems. To see this, let e now be given a positive interpretation as the quality of the environment, so that both sides of (4.9) are positive. Private commodity j can then be interpreted as a measure of the consumer's rate of utilization of the environment, as when improved quality of the water in forest lakes leads to more use of time spent fishing and more expenditure on fishing equipment; in the words of Cropper and Oates (1992) this is an example of the *weak complementarity approach.*

A weakness of the household production approach is that it usually captures only part of the benefits derived by consumers from an improved environment. To return once more to Pigou's example, this method of estimating benefits does not include the aesthetic pleasure of a clearer sky, which is one that does not leave any obvious trace in people's market behaviour, at least not according to this method of observation. The household production approach, if correctly applied, therefore gives a lower bound to the true amount of marginal benefit. However, there is a related approach which pretends to be more complete in this respect. This is the *hedonic price approach,* whose basic idea is that differences in environmental quality are reflected in market prices. The most important areas of application of this approach have been housing, recreation and labour markets. Let us consider briefly the use of housing prices as a source of information about environmental preferences.

We imagine a city or a region with a well-functioning housing market. There is a continuum of house types, differing in size, s, and exposure to environmental pollution, e. Pollution is to be thought of as mainly determined by location, so that the choice of location determines the amount of exposure to pollution. This implies that we may as well think of pollution as a choice variable for the household. The market price of a house is $P(s, e)$, which is increasing in s and decreasing in e; thus, each household demands one house, although houses differ with respect to size

The Estimation of Benefits

and environmental quality.[4] Household utility depends on the consumption of other goods, c, and on the quality-adjusted amount of housing, $h(s, e)$. This expression can be regarded as a special case of the household production function (4.5), and the household optimization problem can be written as

$$\text{Max}_{c,s,e}\, u(c, h(s, e)) \quad \text{s.t.} \quad c + P(s, e) = y.$$

The first-order optimality conditions are

$$(u_h/u_c)h_s = P_s, \tag{4.10}$$

$$(u_h/u_c)h_e = P_e. \tag{4.11}$$

The second of these conditions is of particular interest as showing how environmental quality is reflected in the properties of the price of housing. Since $u_h h_e$ is just the marginal utility of environmental quality, (4.11) shows how one can estimate the marginal willingness to pay on the basis of knowledge about the price function $P(s, e)$, in particular about the functional dependence of P on e. Compared with the household production approach, this method may seem to rest on less restrictive assumptions, since it only requires assumptions about the price function, not about details of household production. However, the inferences to be drawn from information about the price function do rest on a priori assumptions about household preferences and production technology, so that the two approaches in fact are based on very similar foundations. The assumption that environmental quality enters the utility function only through the measure of housing is a restrictive one. People may have preferences for the environment which cannot be captured in this way, which essentially reduces the environment to a private good which can be bought like any other commodity, although in the form of a 'housing package'.

I leave aside the application of this method to the study of labour markets and the working environment (with its interesting connection with the theory of compensating wage differentials) and to the analysis of the demand for recreation. Indirect methods of estimating marginal willingness to pay are based on a solid

---

[4] Alternatively, this could have been written as $P(e)s$, so that the price is to be interpreted as per square metre, adjusted for environmental quality. But analytically this is just a special case of the more general formulation.

foundation in the theory of consumer demand and household production, and they have proved their worth in a number of interesting applications. However, these methods often leave one with the impression that there are important types of benefits that they do not manage to capture. Congestion is bad because it increases your travel time. Air pollution is bad because it may force you to buy a more expensive house but for no other reason. This is a rather narrow concept of environmental attitudes.

4.4. Contingent Valuation

In Section 4.2 above it was pointed out that the method of asking people directly about the benefits that they derive from environmental goods is likely to be unreliable because of the lack of incentives for the respondents to provide truthful answers. At least, this would be the obvious objection to this method from someone approaching environmental issues with a background in public economics, with its strong emphasis on the incentive problems involved in attempts to elicit preferences for public goods. In spite of this, such methods have been given much attention in environmental economics, where they have also come to be of great practical importance. This is especially so in the USA, where they have come to play a role in lawsuits brought by the federal government against firms whose actions have caused serious damage to the natural environment.[5]

A central argument in favour of the contingent valuation method is that it is the only one which in principle could capture all relevant environmental benefits. As already pointed out, the indirect methods suffer from the weakness that they only manage to include the benefits that can be inferred from consumers' behaviour in the market. But some benefits are unlikely to affect behaviour; this is particularly true for those benefits often referred to as non-use or existence values. I may perceive that I have ben-

---

[5] The merits and demerits of the contingent valuation method (or methods) have been discussed in a recent symposium in the *Journal of Economic Perspectives*. An introductory survey of the issues by Portney (1994), which also includes a useful description of the role of contingent valuation in current US environmental policy, is followed by one article (Hanemann 1994) which takes a positive view of this method, and another (Diamond and Hausmann 1994) which is severely critical.

efits from preserving the wildlife in the Antarctic continent. But the fact that I have these preferences can hardly be inferred from my market behaviour, since there is little or anything in my pattern of consumption or time use to indicate that I have these attitudes. If someone wants to find out what my preferences are, there seems to be no alternative but to ask me. And then we are up against the revelation problem, and possibly other problems as well.

The revelation problem has in fact played only a minor role in the debate about the reliability of the contingent valuation method. This may be because a widely recommended (although not always adopted) form of interview is such that on the one hand it manages to stay clear of the freerider problem; on the other hand it does contain an invitation to think about environmental expenditure in a balanced budget context. Still, the method has been a controversial one, and the controversy has been especially heated in the USA, where the method has been proposed as the basis for awarding damages in lawsuits following environmental accidents. A panel appointed by the National Oceanic and Atmospheric Administration (NOAA) in the USA, including some very prominent economists,[6] concluded that the contingent valuation method could in fact be used for this purpose. However, it also pointed out that the method had to be used with a great deal of care; in fact with more care than in the panel's view had been taken in most existing studies. It therefore produced a set of guidelines to be followed in future studies.

The guidelines are to a large extent concerned with the practical design of the interview studies, and these recommendations (stressing e.g. the importance of personal interviews and the need for follow-up questions) need not concern us here. Of particular interest, because it concerns the issue of preference revelation, is the panel's recommendation that people should be asked how they would vote in a referendum on a project promising some environmental benefits, to be financed through higher taxes or product prices. In this case there is hardly any incentive for the respondent to vote against the project simply because he does not want to pay the taxes—unless indeed he genuinely feels that the

---

[6] The composition and recommendations of the panel have been described in Portney (1994).

expenditure is not worth the benefit. On the other hand, he also knows that the project is really going to cost him something, so there is no point in voting in favour if he feels that the benefits are only marginal. Obviously, considerable care has to be taken with the questions and the general design of the survey, so that the answers convey the kind of information that one wants to collect. Survey research is a well-established method in the social sciences, and survey designers have much experience of how to formulate questions so as to ensure maximum reliability of the answers.

The critics of the contingent valuation approach have focused primarily on the respondents' true knowledge of the environmental issues involved in the survey, arguing that the answers hardly have much value if the persons being interviewed have only a vague understanding of what the questions are about. It is difficult to observe the respondents' level of understanding directly, but the critics argue that it shows up in a lack of consistency of valuation in the answers to closely related questions. Examples of this, mentioned by Diamond and Hausmann (1994), are when stated benefits depend on the sequence in which questions are asked, on whether the specific question is grouped together with other questions, or are invariant to the size of the environmental problem that respondents are asked to evaluate. All of these inconsistencies can be found in some of the studies that have actually been carried out, but it should be noted that these did not necessarily conform to the NOAA guidelines.

Another criticism is that respondents often have conceptual difficulties in understanding the concept of willingness to pay. Accordingly, when they state their willingness to pay their answers could primarily be a reflection of their general attitude to environmental problems rather than statements about their personal benefits. Diamond and Hausmann conclude their critical survey of the issues by stating that 'current contingent valuation methods should not be used for damage assessment or for benefit cost analysis' (1994: 63). Instead 'it may be more informative to have expert evaluation of the consequences of an environmental change than to consult the public directly about environmental damage' (ibid. 56).

As pointed out by Hanemann (1994), however, the last statement raises a difficult issue: how are the experts to get their infor-

The Estimation of Benefits

mation about consequences? Take e.g. the case of the environmental consequences of an oil spill. A panel of experts may draw up a list of consequences for, among other things, animal life and the coastal scenery. But if it is a question of developing a cost-benefit calculation for a project intended either to prevent future oil spills or to award damages for past accidents, these physical consequences have to be converted into a money measure. If it is accepted that the valuation involved should be related to consumer preferences, and that consequences of this kind are difficult to evaluate by indirect methods, it is hard to avoid the conclusion that the experts must rely on some kind of contingent valuation method. Perhaps a balanced conclusion would be that the results of contingent valuation surveys should be used as one of several inputs into expert evaluations where important non-use benefits are at stake.

4.5. Demand-Revealing Mechanisms

While the procedures that we have surveyed so far all aim at revealing environmental preferences, none of them tries to elicit individual preferences in a way that mimics the incentive mechanism inherent in markets for private goods. In the case of indirect methods, one utilizes individuals' revelation of preferences for some other purpose, using this to infer something about their environmental preferences. With contingent valuation, one does aim directly at uncovering environmental preferences, but the method does not ensure incentive compatibility; it may not be in the respondents' best interests to reveal their preferences truthfully. The idea of demand-revealing mechanisms in the sense in which it will be used in the present section, is to create an incentive system that will induce individuals to reveal their environmental preferences directly and truthfully, with no direct questioning being involved.

The basic idea of demand-revealing mechanisms was suggested in an article by William Vickrey (1961) on auction theory, apparently a topic that is far removed from the economics of the environment. But, as is often the case in economics, fundamental theoretical ideas turn out to be useful in many different branches of application. Thus, the idea emerged in the public goods context in the 1970s in articles by Clarke (1971), Groves and Ledyard (1977) and several other authors. The contribution of these writers was to show that there exists a tax scheme—sometimes called the Clarke tax—which relates the individual's stated willingness to pay to what he will actually have to pay in such a way that he has private incentives to reveal his true individual preferences; in other words, the tax scheme is incentive compatible. It did not take long before it was realized that this type of mechanism could also be applied to environmental problems; see e.g. Suchanek (1979).[7] A recent contribution by Sinn (1993) combines the Clarke tax with the Pigouvian tax solution, and provides an illuminating discussion of the role that the Clarke tax could play in environmental policy.

The intuition behind the Clarke tax is as follows. Each individual agent is asked to reveal his marginal willingness to pay for a public good. The amount of public goods supply will then be determined by the Samuelson condition that the aggregate marginal willingness to pay, as revealed by the individuals, is equal to the marginal cost. The agent pays a tax which is equal to the total cost of the supply minus the aggregate willingness to pay of all agents *except himself*. If the agent understands the logic of this procedure, he will realize that he indeed has an incentive to tell the truth. Imagine that the agent has somehow decided to reveal the true amount of his marginal benefit and then considers whether to increase his stated amount a little beyond this, i.e. to misrepresent his preferences. What is there to gain? On the one hand, there is the benefit from a slight increase in public goods supply (since this increases with the sum of reported benefits). On the other hand, there will also be a change in the tax. There is a marginal production cost connected with the increased supply, while at the same time there are increased benefits accruing to all other agents. The difference between these is the net social cost of the agent's desire for an increased supply, and this is also the increase in his tax burden. Hence the increase in the agent's tax

---

[7] An interesting early contribution to this literature which is written from a somewhat different perspective, is that of Kwerel (1977). He compared a pure transferable quota system, which gives polluting firms an incentive to overstate their clean-up costs, with a pure effluent charge system, where incentives have the opposite bias. He then devised a scheme combining quotas with subsidies which makes the two incentive distortions cancel each other, implying that firms have been provided with incentives to report their true cost functions.

The Estimation of Benefits

payment is equal to the marginal cost of the increase in supply caused by his misrepresentation of his preferences. But this just proves that the agent's initial state of true reporting is an optimum for him, and by assumption it is also an optimum for society. Just as in perfect markets for private goods, the individual consumer's marginal cost of increased consumption is equal to the alternative cost for society. Hence the Clarke tax has the property that it makes it individually rational for the agent to reveal his preferences truthfully, and it leads to a social optimum in the Samuelson sense.

The application to environmental problems is not difficult to see. It is most direct in the case of public expenditure on collective abatement, which is just an ordinary public good. The model of Chapter 2 showed explicitly that the optimality conditions for public goods and public abatement facilities have the same form and raise exactly the same informational problems; to see this, compare the optimality conditions (2.9) and (2.11), which both involve the equality between aggregate benefits and marginal cost.

An interesting question is whether the insights contained in the demand-revealing mechanisms could be applied to the determination of the optimal Pigouvian tax. Recall that the optimal Pigouvian tax is to be determined via the sum of the marginal environmental benefits, requiring the same type of individual information as public goods. But just as in the case of public goods it is easy to see that individuals do not have the incentives to reveal their true benefits, given that the information is to be used by the government to set the environmental tax rate in accordance with Pigouvian principles. Let us make the same thought experiment as above. Imagine that all agents have stated their true benefits and that the government has set the Pigouvian tax at the optimal level. Imagine further that we give one of the agents the opportunity to change his reported benefit, thereby misrepresenting his preferences. Will he do so? Since the tax rate has already been set so as to be proportional to the sum of marginal benefits, it is also proportional to the *average* marginal benefit. If our agent has a marginal benefit which is *above* the average for the population, and if in addition his level of consumption of the taxed commodity is *below* the average, he clearly has an incentive to increase his reported marginal benefit beyond its true level. Other agents will have similar incentives to misrepresent their true willingness to pay, either in the upward or downward direction, depending on the relative strengths of their consumption and environmental benefits. Evidently, we have to create a more sophisticated mechanism in order to achieve truthful preference revelation.

I shall do this by sketching a model which is similar in its assumptions to that which has dominated the literature in this area. This is notable for assuming a quasi-linear utility function, so that

$$u^i = b^i(x^i, e) + c^i \qquad (i = 1, \ldots n). \tag{4.12}$$

Here c^i is consumption of the *numéraire* commodity, which we should think of as a composite of all other consumption goods, and x^i is the consumption of the commodity that creates the environmental pollution, e. Abstracting from abatement, we can write the environmental damage function simply as

$$e = x = \sum_i x^i. \tag{4.13}$$

Let y^i be the gross income of the consumer and define a^i to be a lump-sum transfer. Then the consumer's budget constraint is

$$(p+t)x^i + c^i = y^i + a^i. \tag{4.14}$$

Substituting from this into the utility function (4.12), we can write net utility as

$$u^i = b^i(x^i, e) - (p+t)x^i + y^i + a^i.$$

The first-order condition for the consumer's optimum, with e being taken as given, is

$$\partial u^i / \partial x^i = \partial b^i / \partial x^i - (p+t) = 0. \tag{4.15}$$

The consumer's optimum is now to be contrasted with the social optimum. Imagine for simplicity that there is a social planner whose welfare function is the sum of individual utilities as given by (4.12); his optimization problem is accordingly

$$\text{Max} \sum u^i \quad \text{s.t.} \quad p \sum_i x^i + \sum_i c^i = R.$$

Here I have assumed that the marginal rate of transformation is constant and equal to p. R is a positive constant representing resource availability. Taking account also of (4.13), the condition for a social optimum becomes

$$\partial b^j/\partial x^j + \sum_i \partial b^i/\partial e = p \qquad (j=1,\ldots,n). \qquad (4.16)$$

From (4.15) and (4.16) we can then conclude that the optimal Pigouvian tax satisfies the condition

$$t = -\sum_i \partial b^i/\partial e. \qquad (4.17)$$

This is just a special case of the more general expression (2.17); like that condition, (4.17) characterizes the optimum on the assumption that the government knows the true marginal willingnesses to pay. But what it in fact knows is only what each consumer reports as his willingness to pay; denote this by $-w^i(e)$ ($w^i(e)$ being the environmental damage, which is a negative number). We have seen that there is no reason to believe that this corresponds to his true benefit, but the government decides that it will use these reported benefits to determine the amount of public goods, so that this will satisfy the condition

$$t = -\sum_i (\partial w^i/\partial e). \qquad (4.18)$$

We now consider the determination of the size of the individual lump-sum transfer. Let us imagine that consumer j is told that he will be paid a subsidy[8] which is equal to the total revenue from the Pigouvian tax minus the contributions offered by all other consumers. We then have that

$$a^j = te + \sum_{i \neq j} w^i = te + \sum_i w^i - w^j \qquad (j=1,\ldots,n). \qquad (4.19)$$

Substituting this expression into the net utility function we then obtain

$$u^j = b^j(x^j, e) - (p+t)x^j + y^j + \left[te + \sum_i w^i - w^j\right]. \qquad (4.20)$$

The determination of the lump-sum subsidy has now been incorporated into the consumer's budget constraint. The consumer

---

[8] The reason that it is most natural to think of the Clarke tax as a subsidy in this case is that the government's project is the introduction of the Pigouvian tax, which creates revenue, not expenditure, for the government. The revenue generated by the Pigou tax is paid back to consumers, at least in part, by the Clarke transfer. In the process, it functions as a reward for truthful revelation of preferences. But the algebraic sign of the transfer is in any case immaterial for the theoretical argument.

finds the level of pollution that will maximize his net benefit; this will have to satisfy the condition that

$$\partial u^j/\partial e = \partial b^j/\partial e + [t + \sum_i (\partial w^i/\partial e) - \partial w^j/\partial e] = 0 \qquad (j=1,\ldots n). \tag{4.21}$$

The first two terms in brackets cancel out because of the government's decision rule (4.18); hence we are left with the condition

$$-\partial b^j/\partial e = -\partial w^j/\partial e \qquad (j=1,\ldots,n), \tag{4.22}$$

and this is just the characterization of truthful reporting: the reported marginal willingness to pay should be equal to the true marginal benefit.

We have now demonstrated how one could create a Clarke–Groves mechanism to reveal the aggregate marginal willingness to pay for environmental improvement in the form of a Pigouvian tax. There are some problems that have been neglected in this treatment, especially that of budget balance for the government. The underlying assumption is that the budget must be balanced by other taxes and transfers, preferably non-distortionary ones; see Groves and Ledyard (1977). But more important in this context is an evaluation of the advantages and drawbacks of the method.

The method shares one important advantage of the contingent valuation method. In principle, it captures the whole of the environmental benefit of the consumer. In one respect it is also a clear improvement on contingent valuation, since the latter offers no guarantee against strategic misrepresentation of preferences. Compared to the indirect methods, it is less restrictive as regards the structure of preferences and the technology of consumption, except for the important fact that it relies on the assumption of quasi-linear utility functions, implying that there are no income effects on environmental benefits.

But the demand-revealing mechanisms also have their disadvantages. The most important is probably that they are difficult to grasp intuitively. I base this judgement primarily on the fact that students invariably find them very difficult to understand. Since students who take a graduate course in public economics should be able to grasp the principles more easily than most, there seems to be a danger that many participants in processes of this kind would have some real difficulties in perceiving that truth-

The Estimation of Benefits 85

telling is really the best strategy, in spite of the theoretical properties that the mechanisms might have. If that is the case, the demand-revealing mechanisms might easily fall prey to problems similar to those connected with contingent valuation methods, since the responders' understanding of the problems as well as the exact nature of the questions asked would be important for the final outcome of the process.

These remarks indicate that the setting up and running of a demand-revealing mechanism might easily become quite costly, and it is perhaps significant that, at least to my knowledge, demand-revealing mechanisms have never been applied to any real-life environmental problem. This does not imply that they never will be, but it does indicate that the development of the mechanisms still has some way to go before they reach the stage of empirical implementation.

Looking back on our review of methods of uncovering preferences for environmental goods, it is clear that no single method can claim to represent the best in the sense of dominating other methods in all respects. At this stage of our knowledge the indirect methods based on the household production approach would seem to offer the safest way to proceed for a number of environmental problems; the assumptions on which they are based are well founded on established theory and can be tested empirically, and the estimation procedures themselves correspond to standard methods of empirical research. But some benefits are difficult to get at by these methods, and one needs to develop further both the method of contingent valuation and that of demand-revealing mechanisms. The inherent difficulty of estimating environmental preferences is a good reason for being open-minded on the issue of methodology.

4.6. Aggregation: From Private to Social Benefits

So far we have mostly considered the estimation of benefits for the single consumer, while for policy decisions it is clear that what we need are estimates of the *social* benefits. The step from individual to social benefits in applied work is not always as explicit as is often assumed in the theoretical literature. For example, in the case of the hedonic price method, estimating environmental benefits from data on house prices implies in any case a reliance on the preferences of a market representative consumer, and it is difficult to disaggregate such measures to obtain estimates of benefits for different individuals or social groups. In the case of a representative consumer, therefore, aggregation consists in multiplying the individual benefit by the number of individuals or households.

Somewhat more generally, the simplest method of aggregating individual benefits is simply to add them up. Thus, if the marginal benefits of a particular environmental measure accrue to five individuals in the amounts (1, 2, 3, 4, 5), then the marginal social benefit is 15, and it is this which should be compared to the marginal cost of the measure. There are at least two ways in which taking the unweighted sum could be justified as the relevant measure of social benefits.

The first and perhaps most obvious is the welfare-theoretic justification. In the analysis in Chapter 2, the first-order conditions for welfare maximization are given by (2.8)–(2.12). (2.10) and (2.11), in particular, showed that the relevant measure of marginal social benefit for the determination of public abatement or Pigouvian taxation was the unweighted sum of individual benefits. These are pure efficiency conditions, and the reason why one could legitimately restrict the estimation of benefits in this way, was the underlying assumption of perfect individualized lump-sum transfers leading to the equalization of marginal social utilities of income across consumers, as summarized in (2.12). But the assumption that such transfers are feasible is of course so strong as to be completely unrealistic. True, there do exist special cases where less perfect transfer mechanisms might involve the neglect of redistributive effects in the assessment of benefits for public goods. As demonstrated by Christiansen (1981), there are cases where an optimal non-linear income tax, in combination with certain separability assumptions, leads to the same result. But if neither of these assumptions apply, the logic of welfare optimization forces us to give up the unweighted sum as the appropriate measure of social benefits. I shall return to this point in the discussion of second-best models in Chapter 5.

Another defence of the method of taking the unweighted sum of benefits is usually associated with Arnold Harberger

The Estimation of Benefits

(1971: 785), who, as one of his three postulates for applied welfare economics, maintained that

[W]hen evaluating the net benefits or costs of a given action (project, program or policy), the costs and benefits accruing to each member of the relevant group (e.g. a nation) should normally be added without regard to the individual(s) to whom they accrue.

Harberger's arguments in favour of this postulate make no reference to the nature of redistribution policy, so it does not hinge on the availability of lump-sum transfers. Rather, the argument is that any deviation from unitary weights involves the economist in value judgements on which he can claim no particular expertise.[9] Moreover, there is a need for professional consensus on the way of doing applied welfare economics, and 'neutrality' in matters involving distributional judgements is according to Harberger a necessary element in such a consensus. A related point of view was expressed by Leif Johansen (1977b), who argued that what he saw as a trend towards making every field of economic policy into 'a battleground in the distributional struggle', could lead to inferior social outcomes. Both the Harberger and the Johansen viewpoints are based on strategic considerations; pushing distributional issues to the foreground of the analysis could in the long run be self-destructive for social welfare.

However, strategic thinking on this issue could also lead to different conclusions. It has often been pointed out that if some elements of a cost-benefit analysis are assessed in quantitative terms whereas others are not, the latter are likely to be neglected by policy-makers. Let us assume that the social benefits of a particular environmental policy have been estimated as equal to the unweighted sum of individual benefits, supplemented by a general but non-quantitative discussion of its distributional impact. Compare that to a study that presents the benefits as a weighted sum for several social groups, with the weights

---

[9] Among other elements in cost-benefit analysis that lie outside the expertise of the economist, Harberger (1971: 785) mentions national defence and natural beauty. Many environmental economists would, however, disagree with this judgement. All of the methods for benefit assessment which we have discussed above should in principle be able to capture the value of natural beauty. This is of course not to deny that the implementation of the theoretical principles would not involve practical difficulties.

depending negatively on average income in the group. Since it is easy to agree with Harberger that economists have no special expertise in determining what the weights should be, it would be sensible for the calculations to be done with several alternative sets of weights in order to show the sensitivity of the outcome to the distributional judgements that could be made. This procedure would have the advantage of showing exactly how distributional judgements interact with efficiency considerations, and it would—perhaps—put the two kinds of considerations on a par as regards the attention they would receive from policy-makers. It is difficult to see that such a procedure would necessarily be in sharp conflict with the idea that there is a need for professional consensus in this type of study. A consensus on method could well exist together with open-mindedness about the precise distributional judgements that would be appropriate in each individual case.[10]

Underlying the whole of this discussion is the assumption that there is *one* distributional problem in society, and that this basically concerns the distribution of utility or welfare. Since individual utility depends on both private consumption and the environment, this implies—as demonstrated in Chapter 2—that the optimal redistribution policy should be carried out through transfer payments, and that environmental policy itself should therefore be distributionally neutral. The basic assumption is that although the impact of environmental degradation could be very different for different individuals or groups, one can always compensate for this by adjusting the amount of the transfer. From this point of view it makes little sense to talk of 'an egalitarian environmental policy'; environmental policy is simply one element of a unified perspective on the distribution of welfare in society.

That this perspective is the only reasonable one to adopt is perhaps not obvious. On the one hand, one could argue that the set of values embedded in this view is consistent with people's behaviour, e.g. such as it is depicted in the indirect methods of benefit assessment. People are willing to live in more polluted environments if house prices are so much lower as to compensate

---

[10] For a further discussion of distributional judgements and welfare weights the reader is referred to Drèze and Stern (1987).

them for it. On the other hand, it is not clear that this observation implies that people would accept it as morally right to receive a direct payment in return for some specific environmental degradation imposed on them by the government. This is discussed in an interesting article by Frey *et al.* (1996), who provide evidence to show that the willingness of local communities to site a nuclear waste repository does not increase when compensation is offered, compared to the case with no compensation. Their explanation is that the notion of selling one's principles for a bribe is morally repulsive to the citizens of the local communities. If such views are representative of attitudes to environmental problems, they raise some serious problems for the welfare-theoretic approach to the estimation of social benefits. However, the authors also argue that moral attitudes may in the long run adjust to the changing economic environment.

This view may also be consistent with a rights perspective on the environment. If people feel they have a inalienable right to a certain quality of the environment, to trade off that right for some material benefit would be seen as an immoral action. However, there are many reasons to believe that what one perceives as rights changes with the technological and social development of society.

One assumption that has been implicit in the discussion so far is that the set of individuals who are exposed to environmental pollution all belong to the same jurisdiction. But there are obviously a number of circumstances in which this is unlikely to be the case. The most obvious is where pollution is transnational, so that some of the victims of pollution belong to another country. In a global view of social welfare the benefits of foreigners ought also to count in the sum of benefits of environmental policy. One could also imagine similar problems arising within a country, where some elements of environmental policy are decided upon in local communities, while the benefits are national or at least with spillover effects to other communities. Particularly in the case of transnational pollution it is easy to feel that the notion of national politicians attempting to maximize a global welfare function becomes very far removed from immediate policy relevance. However, it raises some important problems of international environmental policy coordination, which will be further discussed in Chapter 7.

5   The Tax Structure and the Environment

5.1. The Welfare Economics of Tax Policy

The analysis of taxation as an instrument of environmental policy has so far proceeded on the assumption that there are no other distortions in the economy than those due to environmental externalities. This assumption keeps the analysis as close as possible to the efficiency benchmark of perfect competition, and this is a good analytical strategy if one wishes to develop an intuitive understanding for the exact nature of this type of market failure. On the other hand, the assumption is obviously an unrealistic one, since real economies are full of other distortions that prevent the market system from operating according to the benchmark model. We know from the general theory of the second best, as originally formulated by Lipsey and Lancaster (1956–7), that if there is one set of efficiency conditions that the policy-maker is unable to establish, it will not in general be optimal to try to achieve the remaining ones. This result indicates that our recipes for calculating Pigouvian taxes are likely to be sensitive to assumptions about the existence of other distortions in addition to those stemming from the environmental problems *per se*.

One of the conditions that has to be satisfied for a 'first-best' analysis to be valid is particularly disturbing. This is the assumption that the tax system itself contains no other distortions. This implies either that the revenue from environmental taxes is exactly sufficient to meet the government's requirement for resources to finance public expenditure or that any additional revenue can be raised by means of lump-sum taxes.[1] Neither

---

[1] For completeness we should add that if the environmental tax revenue is more than sufficient for the government's revenue needs, the surplus must be distributed back to consumers in the form of lump-sum transfers.

assumption is attractive. The individual lump-sum taxes required to achieve the first best simply do not exist as a realistic option in tax policy. Instead, all the major forms of taxes and transfers give rise to price distortions and efficiency losses. A more realistic discussion of environmental tax policy should therefore be set in a context of overall system design.

The approach taken in this chapter is that of second-best optimal tax theory in the tradition of Ramsey (1927), Diamond and Mirrlees (1971) and others, which was extended to the case of externalities in Sandmo (1975). The objective of this type of analysis is to characterize the set of taxes that maximizes a social welfare function, subject to a government budget constraint and to a set of restrictions on the availability of tax instruments, notably on the use of lump-sum taxes and transfers.

I do not claim that this is the only sensible approach to the analysis of tax policy. There are those who favour a more positive approach, arguing that economists should strive to explain actual tax policy rather than offer political advice. Attempts to explain the existing tax structure as an equilibrium of a political mechanism are of obvious interest, but they do not invalidate the normative approach. A positive approach should for instance be able to explain how the actual tax system emerges as a compromise between equity and efficiency considerations, but in order to do so it must be able to explain how these considerations should be reflected in the tax system, and this is exactly the purpose of normative theory. The normative approach is simply the economist's contribution towards a more structured debate about the aims and means of tax policy—a debate which is itself a part of the political process. But it should be emphasized that the normative approach has several weaknesses even within its own frame of reference. Of these, the most serious is probably the inadequate account taken of the administrative costs of the tax system. But if we do not pursue the formal models that we know how to handle, it will be very difficult to understand the likely implications of the matters that are left out.

I begin with a model that focuses on issues of efficiency before discussing one which incorporates distributional aspects of taxes and the environment. But before turning to these models it is necessary to reconsider the standard theory of the consumer. Environmental externalities affect not only consumers' welfare but also their behaviour—an important fact which has received relatively little attention in the literature.

5.2. Consumer Behaviour in the Face of Externalities

In the following I shall consider a simplified version of the model introduced in Chapter 2. As far as the individual consumer is concerned, the simplification amounts to the assumption that the vector of private consumption goods is three-dimensional, so that the utility function of the individual consumer can be written as

$$u = u(x_0, x_1, x_2, z, e). \tag{5.1}$$

The consumer chooses his vector of private goods consumption (x_0, x_1, x_2) subject to the budget constraint

$$x_0 + P_1 x_1 + P_2 x_2 = y, \tag{5.2}$$

where y is lump-sum income. This will later be assumed to equal zero, but it is useful to include it at this stage in order to characterize consumer demand functions. Utility maximization leads to the first-order conditions already introduced (as (2.13) in Chapter 2) and accordingly to the demand functions

$$x_j = x_j(P_1, P_2, y, e, z) \quad (j = 0, 1, 2) \tag{5.3}$$

and the indirect utility function

$$v = v(P_1, P_2, y, e, z). \tag{5.4}$$

Partial derivatives of these functions will be denoted by subscripts, so that e.g. $\partial x_1 / \partial P_2$ is written as x_{12} etc.

The functions have the standard properties of consumer demand theory. The Slutsky equations hold in their usual form, and the indirect utility function has the well-known Roy properties. However, these properties are all derived on the assumption of the constancy of e. But since e is generated by the consumption of commodity 2 (which corresponds to commodity J in Chapter 2), it will in fact respond to changes in prices and income as all consumers change their demands. Assuming that all consumers are identical, the environmental damage function that corresponds to (4.13) can be written as

The Tax Structure and the Environment

$$e = Ix_2(P_1, P_2, y, e, z). \tag{5.5}$$

Note the interrelationship between the externality—the amount of environmental pollution—and the demand for commodity 2. Pollution depends on consumption via a relationship that is basically technical (congestion depends on car use, water pollution depends on the amount of emission). But consumption depends on pollution via a demand relationship (the demand for car use depends on congestion; the demand for leisure activities by a lake depends on the quality of the water). To find the effect on pollution of a price change, we differentiate (5.5) to obtain

$$e_k = Ix_{2k}/(1 - Ix_{2e}) \qquad (k = 1, 2). \tag{5.6}$$

The derivative in the denominator is of special interest in expressing the *environmental feedback on demand*. While the numerator gives the aggregate effect of the price change on the demand for commodity 2, holding the environment constant, the denominator takes account of the effect of the changed environment on demand. Assume e.g. that the environmental feedback is negative, as is likely to be the case in traffic congestion. More cars make it less attractive to travel by car. In that case the total effect of a price change on pollution is smaller than the partial effect, i.e. when the environment is assumed to be unchanged. One may think of this as a stepwise process: an increase in the price of car travel, e.g. from the introduction of a toll, reduces travel, but the reduced congestion will then lead to a second-round increase in car travel, so that the final effect is less than the initial effect. As an example of a positive feedback effect, the introduction of a fine for littering the streets will lead to less littering, but the fact that public places are now cleaner may in itself lead to an additional decline in littering. The explanation for this would be that the negative environmental effect of an individual act of pollution has become more noticeable.

Consideration of (5.6) might lead one to think that the total effect of a price change on pollution might not only differ in magnitude from the partial effect; it might even differ in sign. However, it was shown in articles by Cornes (1980) and Sandmo (1980) that for the aggregate demand function to be stable, the feedback effect has to satisfy the condition that

$$-1 < Ix_{2e} < 1. \tag{5.7}$$

This condition will be assumed to hold in the following. The possible non-constancy of the feedback effect (non-linear reaction functions) may lead to cases of multiple demand equilibria with interesting implications for environmental policy; however, these issues will not be pursued here.

Much of the literature on externalities has focused on the special case of *separable externalities*, in which the utility functions can be written as

$$u = u(\varphi(x_0, x_1, x_2, z), e). \tag{5.8}$$

In this case the marginal rates of substitutions between private goods (and also, incidentally, between public and private goods) will be independent of the amount of externality. The same, therefore, will be true of the demand functions, so that the feedback effect vanishes. As pointed out in Chapter 4, under this assumption people *suffer* from environmental pollution, but it does not change the way they *behave*. This may in many cases be a useful simplification, although it is empirically rather restrictive; it is in fact quite hard to think of a case of environmental pollution which does not have some kind of feedback effect. The congestion example has already been mentioned; in addition, air and water pollution influence working conditions, peoples' choice of residential area, their pattern of leisure activities, etc. A static model does not do justice to the complexities of the dynamic structure of the feedback effects which in many cases may be expected to be quite different in the short and in the long run.

In general, going back to the demand and indirect utility functions (5.3)–(5.4) we have that the total effects on demand of changes in income and prices are

$$dx_j/dP_k = x_{jk} + x_{je}e_k \quad (j=0,1,2; k=1,2). \tag{5.9a}$$

$$dx_j/dy = x_{jy} + x_{je}e_y \quad (j=0,1,2). \tag{5.9b}$$

The effects on indirect utility are generalizations of Roy's theorem:

$$dv/dP_k = -\lambda x_k + v_e e_k \quad (k=1,2), \tag{5.10a}$$

$$dv/dy = \lambda + v_e e_y. \tag{5.10b}$$

The effect of increases in prices or income on utility are thus decomposed into the conventional Roy term and an externality term. While the Roy term for prices is necessarily negative (for x_k positive), the externality term may well be positive; this is the case if the price increase leads to less pollution. The Roy term for increased income is positive, but if the increase in income leads to more pollution, there is an additional negative effect on utility. Price and income changes might therefore not only be different in magnitude from the usual case, they might also differ in sign, with price increases leading to higher utility and income increases to lower utility. It is worth stressing that these unconventional effects arise not because of complicated general equilibrium effects, but simply from a consideration of the demand-side interaction between consumers.

5.3. The Optimum Tax Problem

The optimum tax problem for the government is to choose the tax instruments in such a way as to maximize social welfare, subject to a government budget constraint which ensures equality between public sector revenue and expenditure. Private sector behaviour is determined by utility and profit maximization, so that private behaviour acts as a second set of constraints on what is attainable by government policy.

The version of the model with which I shall begin is an extremely simple one. First of all, it is assumed that all consumers are identical, so that the analysis can focus on efficiency, with distributional issues being left aside for the time being. With this assumption the natural choice of a social welfare function is the utilitarian sum of utilities, which we can then write in its indirect form as

$$W = Iv(P_1, P_2, y, e, z). \tag{5.11}$$

On the production side we assume a linear production technology and perfect competition. This implies that producer prices, p_j, are constant. For given producer prices, consumer prices are then determined by the tax rates:

$$P_j = p_j + t_j \quad (j=1,2). \tag{5.12}$$

The government budget constraint requires that net tax revenue equals expenditure on public goods. This can be written as

$$It_1x_1 + It_2x_2 - Iy = p_z z, \tag{5.13}$$

where y is now to be interpreted as a lump-sum transfer from the government to the private sector, and p_z is the producer price of the public good.

It is useful to note that if the government budget constraint is subtracted from the private sector budget constraint (5.2)—the latter having first been multiplied by I—we obtain

$$Ix_0 + Ip_1x_1 + Ip_2x_2 + p_z z = 0,$$

which is simply the aggregate production constraint for the economy as a whole, corresponding to (2.6).

The optimum tax policy ought of course to be considered in conjunction with decisions concerning public expenditure. On the one hand, we cannot determine the optimal tax level without having determined the level of public expenditure. On the other hand, the optimum level of public expenditure should depend on the efficiency costs of taxation. In spite of this, we shall begin by taking the level of public goods supply as given and simply determine the optimal tax structure. This is a legitimate procedure since we shall be concerned with *characterization* of optimal taxes, not with the determination of the tax level. Thus, the results that we shall derive are such as to be valid for any level of public expenditure. Later on we shall consider the interdependence between tax and expenditure policies.

Our problem is one of constrained optimization. To solve it, we write down the Lagrange function

$$L = Iv(P_1, P_2, y, e, z) + \mu(It_1x_1 + It_2x_2 - Iy - p_z z), \tag{5.14}$$

and set its partial derivatives equal to zero.

If we allow the use of the lump-sum transfer as a policy instrument, we are back at the first-best analysis of Chapter 2, although the present formulation is more explicit with respect to the use of policy instruments; indeed, the derivation of policy rules in terms of the actual instruments used rather than in terms of quantities was the great leap forward represented by the use of the duality methods that were introduced in the public economics literature around 1970. For later reference we write down the solution that comes out of the present formulation as

$$t_1 = 0, t_2 = -Iv_e/\lambda, \quad \text{or} \quad \theta_2 = t_2/P_2 = -Iv_e/\lambda P_2. \tag{5.15}$$

The implication is as before that the consumer price of the 'clean' commodity should reflect the marginal cost of production, so there should be no tax. For the 'dirty' commodity the tax rate should be the marginal social damage. This is the dual version of the formula (2.17), with the additional simplification that instead of a proper sum we have multiplication by the number of consumers. The revenue from the Pigouvian tax is unlikely to satisfy the revenue requirement of the government budget constraint, and the implication is that the deficit has to be made up by a lump-sum tax ($y < 0$). Alternatively, should the Pigouvian tax yield an amount of revenue in excess of the requirement, the surplus should be transferred in a lump-sum manner to the consumers (so that $y > 0$).

The first-best policy is mainly of interest as a benchmark for a more realistic treatment of policy options, and we now consider the situation where the lump-sum transfer is not available and the government budget must be balanced by means of distortionary taxes. In a world of identical consumers there would in fact seem to be little reason why a lump-sum tax or transfer should not be a realistic policy instrument, since it would imply that all the identical individuals would pay the same amount of tax. Still, simply as a strategy for better understanding, it is useful to study the case where lump-sum taxation is infeasible, although we stick to the assumption of identical individuals. This procedure enables us to study the efficiency aspects of distortionary taxation in isolation from distributional issues. Later on, the analysis will be extended to the more realistic case of heterogeneous individuals, in which the arguments for the impossibility of lump-sum taxes can be put much more convincingly.

5.4. The Second-Best Tax Structure

From the Lagrangian (5.14) we find that the optimal tax rates must satisfy the first-order conditions

$$t_1(dx_1/dP_1) + t_2(dx_2/dP_1) = [-dv/dP_1 - \mu x_1]/\mu, \tag{5.16}$$

$$t_1(dx_1/dP_2) + t_2(dx_2/dP_2) = [-dv/dP_2 - \mu x_2]/\mu, \tag{5.17}$$

The form of these conditions is familiar to anyone who has studied the theory of optimal taxation; see e.g. Sandmo (1976b). The difference between the present formulation and the standard one lies in the nature of the derivatives of the demand and indirect utility functions, which incorporate the environmental feedback effects.

Substituting into these conditions from the price derivatives (5.9a) and (5.10a), we obtain

$$t_1[x_{11} + x_{1e}e_1] + t_2[x_{21} + x_{2e}e_1] = -\alpha x_1 + (1-\alpha)(-v_e/\lambda)e_1. \quad (5.18)$$

$$t_1[x_{12} + x_{1e}e_2] + t_2[x_{22} + x_{2e}e_2] = -\alpha x_2 + (1-\alpha)(-v_e/\lambda)e_2. \quad (5.19)$$

In addition to using the notation introduced previously, I have defined the parameter α as

$$-\alpha = (\lambda - \mu)/\mu.$$

Equations (5.18–19) look complicated, but they can be simplified. Note first that the two conditions can be seen as a system of linear equations in the tax rates, and one can therefore solve for the taxes either by substitution or by using Cramer's rule. It then turns out that the determinant of the coefficient matrix on the left-hand side of the equations is simply

$$J(1 - Ix_{2e})^{-1},$$

where J is the Jacobian determinant $(x_{11}x_{22} - x_{21}x_{12})$. From (5.7) and standard stability arguments this expression can be taken to be positive.

We may now solve for the tax rate on the clean good to obtain

$$t_1 = \alpha(x_2 x_{21} - x_1 x_{22})/(x_{11}x_{22} - x_{21}x_{12}). \quad (5.20)$$

The remarkable feature of this expression is that it does not reflect the environmental aspects of the problem at all. It is not dependent on the environmental feedback effects on demand, nor does it depend on the marginal social damage. The determinants of the tax rate are the slopes of the demand functions; it is a pure Ramsey tax, designed so as to raise revenue with a minimal loss in terms of efficiency, where efficiency is defined in the usual way, similar to the partial equilibrium calculations of the loss of consumer surplus. This property of the tax on the clean good holds irrespective of its demand relationship with the dirty good.

The pure Ramsey tax interpretation comes out particularly strongly when we make the special assumption, popular in expositions of optimal tax theory, that the demand functions are independent, so that the cross-derivatives vanish; $x_{21} = x_{12} = 0$. Then we may convert the specific tax rate in (5.20) to an *ad valorem* rate by defining $\theta_k = t_k/P_k$ ($k = 1,2$). (5.20) then becomes

$$\theta_1 = \alpha(-1/\varepsilon_{11}). \tag{5.21}$$

Here ε_{11} is the uncompensated elasticity of demand for commodity 1. This is the famous inverse elasticity rule, or rather one version of it; see Sandmo (1987). The efficiency loss from raising tax revenue is less, the less elastic the demand for the taxed commodity is. Hence it follows that from the point of view of efficiency, price-inelastic commodities provide the best tax bases, and the tax rate should be proportional to the inverse of the price elasticity. An interpretation of the economic significance of the proportionality factor α will be given below.

We now solve for the tax on the dirty good, t_2. This can be written as

$$t_2 = \alpha[x_1(dx_1/dP_2) - x_2(dx_1/dP_1)](1 - Ix_{2e})/(x_{11}x_{22} - x_{21}x_{12}) + (1-\alpha)(-Iv_e/\lambda). \tag{5.22}$$

Note that the form of this equation is that of a weighted average, the weights being α and $(1 - \alpha)$. The second term in the average formula is evidently the marginal social damage. The first term in the average depends, like the formula (5.20) for t_1, on the slopes of the demand functions, only that in this case the demand functions are inclusive of the environmental feedback effects. Again, to bring out the essence of the economic interpretation, it is instructive to examine a special case. To construct the special case I make two simplifying assumptions. First, I assume that externalities are separable as in (5.8); this implies that the environmental feedback effects vanish. Second, I assume, as in the discussion of the tax on the clean good, that demand functions are independent, so that $x_{21} = x_{12} = 0$. (5.22) then becomes, when converted into an *ad valorem* form

$$\theta_2 = \alpha(-1/\varepsilon_{22}) + (1-\alpha)(-Iv_e/\lambda P_2). \tag{5.23}$$

The tax rate should be a weighted average of the inverse elasticity and the marginal social damage. Note that the weight given to the first of these terms is the same as the proportionality factor in the formulae for the optimal tax on the clean good, (5.20) and (5.21).

To interpret the two sets of formulae, note that if $\alpha = 0$, we get back to the first-best solution (5.15). No distortionary taxes are being used to raise revenue, so that in this case we have the happy coincidence that the revenue from the Pigouvian tax alone, when set at its first-best level, is exactly sufficient to satisfy the government's revenue requirement. To be able to achieve the first-best allocation of resources without lump-sum taxes or transfers is of course more than one can realistically hope for. If α is 'low', we have an approximation to this solution, but on the other hand it is not quite clear what this means.

To get a better understanding of this case, consider now the opposite case where $\alpha = 1$. Now the weight on the Pigouvian term vanishes, and the tax rates on both the clean and the dirty good should be equal to their inverse elasticities.[2] But this obviously corresponds to the case of maximal tax revenue; the revenue requirement has been set at a level corresponding to the top of the Laffer curve. There is no scope then for having environmental concerns reflected in the tax structure; the tightness of the government's budget constraint simply does not allow it. But observe from the general expression (5.22) that although the *evaluation* of the environment is absent from the tax formula in this when $\alpha = 1$, the *behavioural effect* of a changing environment is relevant for the calculation of the revenue-maximizing tax rate. From this discussion it follows that the empirically relevant and interesting case is where $0 < \alpha < 1$; tax rates are positive, but less than the rates that would maximize revenue.

There are two main conclusions that can be drawn from this analysis. The first is that the system of commodity taxes can be seen as consisting of two components, one revenue-raising (the Ramsey component) and one environmental (the Pigou component). The environmental term is only present in the tax formula for the dirty good, whereas taxes on clean goods should be set according to standard optimum tax considerations. This 'targeting' of the tax system is the essence of the first-best solution, and

---

[2] This refers to the special case of demand independence, but the nature of the argument is exactly the same for the more general case.

it is interesting to note that it carries over to the second-best framework. The second conclusion is that the weights accorded to the two terms should reflect the tightness of the government's budget constraint. The higher is the government's revenue requirement, relative to the maximum attainable, the less is the weight of the environmental term as a determinant of the tax on the dirty good.

Two comments are in order at this point. As to the first conclusion, it should be kept in mind that the tax formulae derived are characterization results and not closed-form solutions; the significance of the weighted average formula—or the additivity property, as it was called in Sandmo (1975)—therefore should not be exaggerated. The two terms as well as the weights are results of the same optimization process. Still, the formulae suggest a fruitful way of thinking about the two objectives of tax policy in the present model, viz. to raise revenue with a minimum of distortionary loss and to correct a market failure.

With regard to the second conclusion, it is worth noting that it appears to go against an argument sometimes heard in public debates about green taxation to the effect that environmental taxes become more important, the higher is the tax level. The reasoning behind this argument is presumably that the higher the tax level is, the more distortionary it tends to become, and the more essential it is to utilize the non-distortionary options of tax policy. I do not in fact think that there is necessarily anything wrong with this argument, but it should be kept in mind that it is usually advanced without any careful statement of the underlying assumptions. In the case analysed here, the conclusion is based on a highly specific set of assumptions, notably that the tax system has been chosen optimally.[3] The popular argument, by contrast, seems to refer to some situation where environmental taxes, in the initial state of policy, have for some reason not been used at all. To argue that efficiency gains can be made by starting to use them, seems indeed to be sensible. What the present conclusion tells us is that the popular argument is not necessarily correct, and that the assumptions on which it builds should be examined carefully. This is a good example of the contribution

---

[3] The same assumption underlies the influential analysis of Bovenberg and de Mooij (1994); see also the comment by Fullerton (1997).

that optimal tax theory can make to what Frank Hahn (1973) has called 'the grammar of policy arguments'.

5.5. Second-Best Taxes: Heterogeneous Consumers and Distributional Concerns

I have already remarked on the artificial nature of an analysis which on the one hand assumes that all individuals are equal in terms of personal characteristics and on the other hand that lump-sum taxation is infeasible. For in the case of identical individuals an optimal lump-sum tax would take the form of a head tax, with an equal amount to be paid by all, and this would be as simple, efficient and equitable a tax system as one could wish. But when, as is the case in reality, consumers differ with respect to their productivities and preferences, a policy of optimal lump-sum taxes and transfers would have to be individualized, and this would require much more information about individuals than the government could possibly have. For example, if the government can only observe consumers' earning power via their incomes, as assumed in the optimal income tax literature, a tax on income distorts individuals' choices between labour and leisure. The conclusion to be drawn from this is that tax design under second-best conditions must take account not only of efficiency but also of distributional aspects of the tax system.

In a model that takes account of differences between individuals, one must have some idea about the source of these differences. In the Mirrlees (1971) optimal income tax model, individuals are assumed to have different productivities which are translated directly into wage differences via a competitive labour market. But this is not the only alternative; thus, in Sandmo (1993) I have explored a model where people differ in their preferences with respect to work and leisure. Since on the present occasion I want to concentrate on basic principles, I simply assume that each consumer has a personal characteristic, represented by the parameter κ^i, which enters his indirect utility function, which we now write as

$$v^i = v(P_1, P_2, y, e, z, \kappa^i). \tag{5.24}$$

The indirect utility function emerges from the maximization of the direct utility function subject to the budget constraint. Therefore, the parameter κ^i could come from either preferences or market opportunities and is consistent with several assumptions with respect to the sources of inequality.

The social welfare function I take for simplicity to be the utilitarian sum of utilities, so that

$$W = \sum_i v^i. \qquad (5.25)$$

The optimal tax problem is to maximize (5.25) subject to the budget constraint, which now must be written as

$$t_1 X_1 + t_2 X_2 = p_z z. \qquad (5.26)$$

In this formulation the upper-case X_k stands for the total quantity consumed of commodity k; $X_k = \Sigma x_k^i$ (k = 1,2).

We can now rewrite the optimal tax problem in the format used before and derive the characterization of the optimal solution. Since the point here is not to present the result in the most general form possible, but simply to show how distributional concerns modify the previous result, I concentrate on the simplified case of separable externalities and demand independence. The optimum tax formulae can then be written as

$$\theta_1 = \delta_1(-1/\varepsilon_{11}), \qquad (5.27)$$

$$\theta_2 = \delta_2(-1/\varepsilon_{22}) + \sum_i (1-\alpha^i)(-v_e^i/\lambda^i P_2). \qquad (5.28)$$

The formal similarity to the pure efficiency characterization is obvious; in particular, the additive structure of the optimal tax formulae still holds. However, there are also some significant modifications. First of all, the weight given to the inverse elasticity term in the two formulae now differ between the two commodities. The weights are defined by

$$\delta_k = \sum \alpha^i x_k^i / \sum x_k^i \qquad (k = 1,2), \qquad (5.29)$$

where $\alpha^i = -(\lambda^i - \mu)/\mu$, and δ_k is the *distributional characteristic* of commodity k. To see the justification for this terminology, note that α^i differs between individuals because they have different marginal utilities of income. With our utilitarian social welfare function λ^i is the social marginal utility of income for individual i. Accordingly, the distributional characteristic is a weighted average of a scaling of the social marginal utility of income. It takes a low value if the consumption of commodity k is concentrated among people with a high social marginal utility of income and a high value in the opposite case. Thus, in the case of commodity 1, the clean good, the tax should be lower, the more elastic is the aggregate demand function *and* the lower is the distributional characteristic. In the case of commodity 2, the dirty good, the Ramsey part of the optimum tax rate should be computed according to the same principles.

From (5.28) it also follows, however, that the distributional concerns should enter into the second or Pigouvian part of the tax formula as well. If a high valuation of the environment tends to be concentrated among those with a high social marginal utility of income, this will tend to increase the Pigouvian term. The formulation here is very general, but for particular applications we might think of people with high and low social marginal utility of income as being the poor and the rich, respectively. If the consumption of the rich imposes a serious environmental damage on the poor, this will, in a society committed to egalitarian values, make an especially strong case for a high rate of tax on the dirty good. The tax burden falls chiefly on the rich, while the environmental benefit accrues to the poor. But this is not the only possible constellation of benefits and costs, and the manner in which an environmental tax should combine equity and efficiency considerations must be determined in each particular case.

In more general terms this analysis has important implications for one's view of the connection between distributional and environmental policy. A common objection to indirect taxation in general is that it is likely to be regressive, and this objection is also sometimes heard in debates about environmental taxes. However, it should be kept in mind that the incidence effects of environmental taxes are different in principle from that of other taxes. I have already stressed the point that price increases on 'dirty' goods may in fact be beneficial to the consumers via their effects on environmental quality. In effect, when we think of the environment as a public good, the provision of which can be changed by government tax policy, the Pigouvian tax has some of the characteristics of an earmarked tax; its welfare effects cannot be separated from those of the public good benefits that it creates. The redistributional effects of environmental taxes should therefore be evaluated simultaneously with the incidence of the benefits.

The imperfect matching between instruments and targets that is illustrated by the formal analysis of optimal second-best tax models should not blind us to the fact that there may be other reasons why such a matching might be a good idea in practical policy-making. It becomes easier to determine optimal Pigouvian taxes if one's thinking can be limited to efficiency considerations. This assumes of course, that there are other policy instruments, like direct taxation and the social security and social assistance systems, that are better suited—even if not perfectly suited—to handle the distributional problem. Although I personally find this idea to be an appealing one, I must also admit that there are cases where it is not easy to stick to this principle. One is where environmental taxes have very strong regional incidence effects, threatening e.g. to create heavy local unemployment. Although national benefits may argue in favour of heavy environmental charges on the local producers, concern for the standard of living of the local population may lead to a more cautious policy of gradual reform.

5.6. The Tax Base

In Chapter 1 (Section 1.6) I discussed briefly some of the problems that arise with the choice of the proper base for environmental taxes. The ideal tax base is the one that coincides perfectly with the source of the particular environmental pollution. If pollution is due to factory smoke, as in the example from Pigou (1920) that I have already cited, then the ideal tax base is the amount of smoke, not the amount of fuel burned in the ovens nor the volume of the output for which the fuel is used. If water pollution comes from the emission of a particular chemical substance, then it is the amount of that substance which should be taxed, not the total amount of waste of which the substance is a part, and not the volume of production of which the waste is a by-product. The general principle is that one wishes to create a substitution away from the harmful activity with as few additional substitution effects as possible.

This ideal is not always attainable, and the problem is essentially one of imperfect observability. It may be feasible to tax smoke emissions, but the costs involved in monitoring and measurement may be high; consequently, one has to consider whether the gains from a better tax base are high enough to justify the monitoring costs. In the model discussed in the present chapter we have looked at a case where pollution is due to the consumption of some market commodity, and in such a case the tax base is no different from that of any kind of indirect taxation. In the model, taxing the source of pollution is equivalent to taxing the sales or purchases of the 'dirty good'. When interpreting the theory with a view to practical application, one should, however, keep the tax base problems in mind so as not to suggest policies that may have serious adverse side-effects. The problems involved in targeting the tax base to the objectives of environmental policy have obvious counterparts in the use of quantitative regulations; there too, the choice of what to regulate must take account both of the accuracy involved and the costs of monitoring.

Some attempts have in fact been made to model problems of this kind. I have already mentioned (in Chapter 2.2) the work by Diamond (1973) in which consumers' marginal contributions to environmental damage differ from each other, but where individual taxation is impossible. In Sandmo (1976a) I studied the case where the same market commodity is used by households as an input into two different household production processes, only one of which generates environmental externalities. The principle of ideal targeting then calls for taxing only the harmful use of the commodity, but if the government can only observe total purchases, such a differential tax becomes impossible. (It makes no sense to ask drivers to what extent they intend to use the petrol that they buy for driving in congested or highly polluted areas.) By imposing a tax on the dirty good (which is really only partially dirty) one does in fact achieve an efficiency gain in the form of an improved environment, but at the same time one introduces an additional substitution effect which from an efficiency point of view is undesirable.

An important insight derived from the study of this model is that the additivity property which was so much emphasized above, no longer holds. In other words, there might be a case for environmentally motivated taxes on clean goods. A tax on the 'innocent' part of the dirty good creates an undesirable substitution effect in the direction of reduced consumption. By taxing commodities that are substitutes for the clean use or complements with the dirty use one achieves an efficiency gain. A tax on petrol will reduce air pollution. But if air pollution is only a problem in the city centre, the policy may be improved by introducing parking fees in the centre, even when there is no shortage of parking space.[4]

5.7. Tax Theory and Policy

Having been through a number of technicalities, we may well ask whether optimum tax theory has anything substantial to contribute to the policy debate about environmental taxation. The answer to this question depends upon one's view of the basic role of such a theory. If you take the view that optimum tax theory ought to provide a set of formulas into which economists in the Ministry of Finance can feed their numbers, I believe that you will be frustrated. If, on the other hand, you see the role of theory as providing guidelines for clear thinking about policy, then you should find this type of theorizing to be useful. It is e.g. not obvious in a second-best situation that one should not recommend the imposition of Pigouvian taxes on goods that are complements to the 'dirty' goods and subsidies on the substitutes—but the theory tells us we should not do so except under particular circumstances. Neither is it obvious that the computation of the marginal social damage itself remains basically the same as in the first-best case; in particular, the assessment of the marginal social damage does not vary with the price elasticity of demand for the 'dirty' good.

An important feature of normative tax theory is the sensitivity of the optimal solution to the assumptions made about the availability of tax instruments. This emerges with special clarity in the contrast between the first-best and second-best cases discussed above, but the point is in fact more general, as was also brought out in the discussion of the tax base. The design of the tax system should be seen as a whole, and the environmental tasks of the tax system must be seen in connection with its other tasks of raising revenue and redistributing income. The formal theory of optimal taxation has less to say about the optimal set of tax instruments

---

[4] Local air pollution is not the only environmental effect of petrol consumption, and the global warming effects call for effective taxation of petrol in all uses. But the basic point of the example is independent of this complication.

to use than about the optimal use of the set of taxes once it has been selected, so that the analytical formulation of the optimal tax problem often has to reflect a prior choice on what is empirically relevant and realistic.[5]

Another feature of the theory which deserves special emphasis is the sensitivity of optimal taxes to the distributional objectives of the government. In the utilitarian optimum discussed in Section 5.5, the social welfare function is the sum of individual utility functions. These are derived from the consumers' ordinal preferences, but to construct the social welfare function, the government must choose a special cardinal form of the utility functions. If the government is inequality averse, it will choose a cardinal transformation so as to yield a decreasing marginal utility of income. How concave the transformation is, will determine the variation of the marginal utility of income among consumers as well as the distributional characteristics δ_k. This will in turn determine the structure of indirect taxes and the balance between revenue-raising, redistributional and environmental concerns in the taxes on dirty goods.

---

[5] Formally, the problem is essentially one of non-convexities in the administrative costs of the tax system. It is e.g. more costly to have a highly differentiated system of indirect taxes than a uniform one, but once a differentiated system is in place, the costs are probably not very sensitive to the degree of differentiation. Having one VAT rate of 15% is less costly than having one of 10% and one of 20%, but the latter system is not likely to be more expensive than one where the rates are 7% and 23%.

6 The Double Dividend and the Marginal Cost of Funds

6.1. Indirect Benefits of Environmental Taxation

The analysis of Chapter 5 emphasized the point that environmental taxes, in raising revenue for the government, must be considered a part of the general tax system of society; tax policy should be seen as an integrated whole. How much weight should be given to environmental taxes must then depend on the government's revenue needs. This conclusion emerges directly from an interpretation of the conditions for second-best optimality of the tax system.

Two points of view have been important in recent discussions about environmental tax reform. The first is that environmental taxation has not yet had the impact on tax policy that it should; too few opportunities for improving the quality of the environment through green taxes have so far been exploited. The other is that with the present high levels of public expenditure and taxation in modern societies, the distortionary costs of taxation have become very high. Making more use of environmental taxes, which promise efficiency gains instead of losses, could bring the cost of tax distortions substantially down. From these two views there emerges the first version of what has become known as 'the double dividend hypothesis'. According to this hypothesis, the introduction of environmental taxes and subsequent increases in tax revenue allow governments to reduce other, distortionary taxes. This leads to a reduction in the overall efficiency loss from taxation, and when this is set beside the environmental gain, we have a double dividend from environmental taxes. The conclusion seems eminently sensible. As we shall see, however, when we try to make it more precise, the hypothesis is not quite as obvious as it may first appear.

During the last couple of decades unemployment has reemerged as one of the major economic and social issues of our time. It is only to be expected, therefore, that any proposal for new taxes should be judged in terms of their effect on unemployment. A natural idea is that by relying more on environmental taxes it should be possible to reduce taxes on employment and thereby increase the demand for labour, which in turn should lead to less unemployment. This is the second version of the double dividend from a green tax reform. Compared to the previous version of the double dividend, this is different in that the distortion to be removed is not one that is primarily due to the tax system. It is also different in being more visible. One does not have to introduce politicians to the world of shaded triangles to convince them of the importance of reduced unemployment.

These two versions of the double dividend hypothesis rely on what has become known as 'revenue recycling'—an environmentalist term for tax reform. The basic idea is that by more use of environmental taxes other taxes can be cut, and this can lead to other, non-environmental gains. Underlying the analysis is the assumption that tax revenue is to be held constant. One may argue that this is a natural analytical assumption, since the issue of the size of the public sector is a separate one. But is it? One measure of the efficiency cost of distortionary taxes which has received a lot of attention in recent years is the marginal cost of public funds (MCF). This is a measure of how costly it is to raise an additional amount of tax revenue when account is taken of the distortionary costs of higher tax rates. If environmental taxes really lead to a less distortionary tax system, then a green tax reform should lower the MCF relative to what it otherwise would have been. But if that happens it would be rational to expand the public sector. This too is a kind of extra dividend; it is one way in which to reap the gains from a more efficient tax system. On the other hand it has been claimed in the literature that it is not obvious that a green tax reform will in fact lower the marginal cost of public funds, so that this matter too needs closer investigation.

In the rest of this chapter I go into more detail about each of these three ideas of non-environmental gains from a green tax reform.

6.2. The Double Dividend: A Better Environment and a More Efficient Tax System

Although this version of the double dividend hypothesis seems so obviously right, some further thought will easily convince us that there are nevertheless some complications ahead. The important issue is the choice of an initial situation from which to judge the result of a green tax reform. Suppose that we were in a situation where the tax system could be characterized by equations (5.20) and (5.22), so that taxes are optimal in a second-best sense. Starting from this situation, is it possible to imagine a welfare-increasing green tax reform? The answer is obviously no, and the reason is simple. Because the tax system is already optimal, any balanced-budget reform can only decrease welfare. It is possible that a reform could be found that would improve the environment, but this would necessarily be more than offset by an increase in the distortionary costs of the tax system.

Once the point has been made, it is obvious that a second-best optimum is not an interesting initial situation from which to judge the double dividend hypothesis. Instead of looking at it from the optimal taxation or *tax design* viewpoint, we ought to consider it from the point of view of *tax reform*. The distinction between the two, which was first emphasized by Feldstein (1976), is that the problem of tax design is to characterize the best of all available tax systems, whereas in the analysis of tax reform our more modest ambition is to judge whether a change in the tax system, starting from some historically determined initial situation, will increase welfare.

A more detailed analysis will make the issues clearer. So as not to make matters too complicated, I go back to the economy with identical individuals. To simplify the mathematics I also assume that externalities are separable in the utility function, so that there are no environmental feedbacks on demand.

The social welfare function is as before

$$W = Iv(P_1, P_2, y, e, z), \qquad (6.1)$$

where the environmental damage function can now, because of the separability assumption, be written as

$$e = Ix_2(P_1, P_2, y, z). \tag{6.2}$$

A tax reform will change the prices and thereby affect the environment. Lump-sum transfers, however, are ruled out, and the supply of public goods is taken as constant. Taking the differential of the social welfare function, we obtain

$$dW = I(-\lambda x_1 + v_e Ix_{21})dP_1 + I(-\lambda x_2 + v_e Ix_{22})dP_2. \tag{6.3}$$

We can now write the change in welfare in units of the *numéraire* as

$$dW^* = dW/\lambda = I(-x_1 - mx_{21})dP_1 + I(-x_2 - mx_{22})dP_2. \tag{6.4}$$

Here I have introduced the symbol m to denote the marginal social damage, so that, formally,

$$m = -Iv_e/\lambda.$$

Obviously, $m > 0$. Let $R(t_1, t_2)$ be the government's tax revenue, and let R_1 and R_2 be its partial derivatives. The public sector's budget constraint is

$$R(t_1, t_2) = It_1 x_1 + It_2 x_2 = p_z z. \tag{6.5}$$

A tax reform must satisfy the requirement that government revenue is constant. Taking the differential of (6.5), this implies that

$$R_1 dt_1 + R_2 dt_2 = 0. \tag{6.6}$$

Using this to eliminate dt_1, we can substitute back into the welfare differential[1] and write the welfare effect of a balanced budget tax reform as

$$dW^*/dt_2 = [x_1(R_2/R_1) - x_2] + [x_{21}(R_2/R_1) - x_{22}]m. \tag{6.7}$$

This expression splits the welfare change into two terms. The first of these represents the welfare change that would emerge from a tax reform, *even if there had been no externalities*. Remember that we have a distortionary tax system and that we start with an arbitrary set of tax rates (except for the fact that they satisfy the government budget constraint). An increase in the tax rate on commodity 2 combined with a lowering of the rate on commod-

---

[1] Recall that $dP_k = dt_k$ for k = 1, 2.

ity 1 will in general have an effect on the efficiency of the system, quite apart from its effect on the environment.[2] But whether the effect will be positive or negative is so far an open question. The second term is proportional to the marginal social damage, but the factor of proportionality depends on the demand functions in a way which makes it less than obvious that it is positive.

So far we may conclude that we can indeed identify two conceptually separate dividends from a green tax reform, the first of which is a conventional tax efficiency dividend while the second is an environmental dividend. But we have not yet determined whether the dividends are guaranteed to be positive. Before looking into this in more detail, it is worth going back to the point mentioned previously: At the optimum which we identified in the previous chapter it must be the case that $dW^*/dt_2 = 0$. It is worth checking to see if this is indeed the case.

By manipulating the optimum tax conditions (5.16) and (5.17), we find, using also equations (5.10a) and (5.6) for the separable case, that they can be rewritten as

$$R_k = I(\lambda/\mu)(x_k + mx_{2k}) \qquad (k = 1, 2). \tag{6.8}$$

It follows that

$$R_2/R_1 = (x_2 + mx_{22})/(x_1 + mx_{21}). \tag{6.9}$$

Inserting this expression back into (6.7) it follows after some simple manipulations that it is indeed the case that the gain from a marginal green tax reform is zero. This is an application of the envelope theorem: at the optimum all gains and losses from changes in the tax structure have been perfectly balanced. This is obviously not meant to be a startling new insight but rather a proof that our model of the gains from tax reform has been correctly constructed.

There is a bit more to the result than this, however. Suppose that we were in an initial situation where there was no environmental pollution, or, alternatively, where people were not aware of its existence. In fact, many of the environmental problems that concern us today were completely unknown to the majority of

---

[2] That there could be a gain from a green tax reform even if environmental considerations are disregarded follows from the general theory of tax reform, but in the context of the double dividend debate this point acquires a special significance; see Goulder (1995).

people only a few decades ago, so that this thought experiment has some claim to realism. Suppose further that in this situation an enlightened government had optimized the tax system, although under the assumption that $m = 0$. Now an environmental shock occurs, either in the real world or in people's minds, and the government realizes that there is now a case to be made for a reform that raises the tax on the dirty good. Let us assume that this creates an environmental dividend. What about the tax efficiency dividend? Given the assumption that the tax system had previously been chosen according to the Ramsey criterion, there is no efficiency gain. There is a single, not a double dividend.

Technically, the last point can be demonstrated by noting that when $m = 0$, (6.9) implies that $R_2/R_1 = x_2/x_1$ at the optimum. Substituting this into (6.7) it follows that the first dividend is zero.

So far we have shown that there exist certain initial states of the tax system from which a reform yields either no dividend at all or only a single, environmental dividend. It is time to look further at the more general case and see if it is likely that a green tax reform will in fact result in two positive dividends. This easily becomes very complicated. In order to avoid too much analytical detail, I shall make the additional assumption that in the initial state the marginal tax revenues R_1 and R_2 are positive. This means that the tax rates are each on the upward-sloping segments of their 'Laffer curves'. This empirical assumption seems quite reasonable, and it also corresponds to the assumption usually made, although implicitly, in policy discussions of green tax reforms. Both politicians and economists tend to take for granted that if you raise taxes on dirty goods and lower them on clean goods you will in fact increase revenue from the former source and lower revenue from the latter.

Now consider the first dividend again, the one that describes *tax revenue efficiency*. We have seen that this is zero in a Ramsey optimum. But this means that if in the initial situation the tax on the dirty good is below its Ramsey value, there must be a gain in tax revenue efficiency, and thus a positive dividend. Conversely, if t_2 were initially higher than its Ramsey value, the dividend would be negative. Since in general there can be no presumption that the initial tax rate on the dirty good is either below or above its Ramsey value, it is not possible to claim theoretical support for the position that the first dividend is necessarily positive. This depends on the initial state of the tax system.

It is possible to be a bit more precise about the condition for the tax efficiency dividend to be positive. To do this, we substitute the derivatives of the demand functions into the expressions for the marginal tax revenues, use the Slutsky equations and manipulate the expressions along the lines described in e.g. Sandmo (1987). Then we find that for the tax efficiency dividend to be positive, we must have

$$\theta_2/\theta_1 < (\sigma_{11} + \sigma_{22} + \sigma_{20})/(\sigma_{11} + \sigma_{22} + \sigma_{10}), \qquad (6.10)$$

where θ_1 and θ_2 are the *ad valorem* tax rates and σ_{jk} are the compensated price elasticities. This condition was first derived by Corlett and Hague (1953–4). To see its implications, assume that the initial state of the tax system is one of uniformity, so that $\theta_1 = \theta_2$. Then (6.10) says that the reform will improve tax revenue efficiency if and only if $\sigma_{20} < \sigma_{10}$, so that the dirty good is the more strongly complementary with the *numéraire* good.[3]

Although simple, this is a very abstract condition. Can it be interpreted in ways which have a stronger appeal to one's intuition about practical tax reform proposals?

Corlett and Hague referred to the untaxed commodity 0 as 'leisure'. Most economists would in fact argue that leisure is subsidized via the personal income tax. One way to think of the case studied here is as a reform of the system of indirect taxes, given that there exists an income tax which is not included in the programme for reform. This might be because politicians feel that the role of the income tax for the redistribution of income is so important that it should not be mixed up in the discussions of green tax reform. If this is the case, there is a fixed distortion in the labour market which taxes labour and subsidizes leisure. By raising taxes on goods which are complementary with leisure, one discourages the consumption of the subsidized commodity and so moves the leisure–consumption pattern of consumers, which is being distorted by the tax system, back in the direction of the first-best

---

[3] Or, to spell it out in more detail, the condition is satisfied if either (i) commodities 0 and 1 are substitutes while 0 and 2 are complements, (ii) both 1 and 2 are substitutes for 0, but 2 is the weaker substitute, (iii) both 1 and 2 are complements with 0, but 2 is the stronger complement. The formulation in the text is intended as a compact version of this more complex statement.

allocation of resources. Raising taxes on transport activities, many of which contribute heavily to environmental problems, is likely to yield a positive tax efficiency dividend if, in an economy of high marginal taxes on labour, they discourage leisure. But if instead they discourage labour through increased costs of labour-force participation, their tax efficiency dividend in a green tax reform is more likely to be negative.[4]

So far we have demonstrated that it is very difficult to say anything very precise about the sign and extent of the first dividend from an environmental tax reform—the tax efficiency dividend. In order to say with confidence that it is positive and of significant magnitude, we need to make further assumptions both about the initial state of the tax system and about the demand interrelations between the various taxed goods. This should come as no surprise to anyone familiar with second-best tax analysis.

Now consider the second term in (6.7), the *environmental dividend*. It is natural to assume that the demand curve for the dirty good is downward-sloping, so that $x_{22} < 0$. Then a sufficient condition for the environmental dividend to be positive is that $x_{21} > 0$; the dirty and clean goods must be gross substitutes. The economic intuition behind this result should be clear. The tax reform increases the price of the dirty good. The resulting fall in consumption leads to a direct environmental improvement. At the same time the price of the clean good falls. Because the goods are substitutes, this reinforces the direct effect, leading to a further environmental improvement. Note that substitutability between the two goods is sufficient but not necessary for this conclusion. It is only the case of strong complementarity between the two goods that leads to the possibility of a negative environmental dividend. If we think of the clean and dirty goods as representing broad groups of commodities and of the tax reform as a general shift of the tax base in the direction of dirty goods, it seems most realistic to think of the two groups as substitutes and therefore to believe that the environmental dividend is indeed positive.

We have seen that it is possible to decompose the welfare gain from a green tax reform in a revenue efficiency and an environmental dividend. This is a useful way to organize one's thoughts

---

[4] For a more general analysis of the conditions for a tax reform to be welfare improving see Dixit (1975).

The Marginal Cost of Funds

about the gains from a reform. However, we have also seen that economic theory does not give unqualified support to the view that both dividends will be positive. Although this is likely to be the case for the environmental dividend, no strong case can in general be made for the tax revenue dividend to be positive. However, the agnostic conclusion does not mean that it is useless to think about a green tax reform from the double dividend point of view. All it means it that the signs and magnitudes of the dividends are basically matters to be clarified by empirical research, and they have to be assessed for each individual reform proposal. In this sense the theory cannot provide definite conclusions, but it does provide an analytical framework for thinking about the issues.

6.3. Boosting Employment: Another Dividend?

The formal models that we have been using all rely on the assumption that markets are cleared by prices. When markets and prices are given an interpretation in terms of labour and wages, the assumption must therefore be that this is also the case for the labour-market. The supply of labour is equal to demand; by assumption, therefore, there can be no unemployment in this type of model. From the point of view of standard welfare economics, whether a tax reform increases or decreases employment is of secondary importance for the analysis. The amount of employment—of labour-force participation and hours worked—has no special significance; leisure is simply another consumer good, and labour time is the part of the endowment of leisure which is sold in exchange for other consumer goods.

In order to come to grips with the interrelationship between environmental policy and unemployment we must therefore adopt a different analytical approach. In order to choose among the many models that claim to present good explanations for unemployment, we would have to engage in a far-reaching survey of the modern theory of labour economics. But this would take us too far away from our main theme, and I shall simply choose one type of model which is both tractable and relevant. This is the so-called monopoly union model, where there is a trade union which sets wages. Firms in turn take wages as given and hire labour as in the standard neoclassical model. But at the wages set by the union, there will be an excess supply of workers who cannot get jobs; hence there is unemployment. A very clear exposition of this type of model is that of Oswald (1985), and I shall take this as my point of departure. How well the model explains the actual extent of unemployment is an open question. My own judgement is that it provides a central element in the explanation of European unemployment, while it may be less relevant for the US economy, where trade unions are generally considered to be much less powerful.[5]

The microeconomic framework will in some ways be simpler than in the previous section. Every employed person is assumed to supply one unit of labour, and for this they receive the wage w. The unemployed receive an unemployment benefit in the amount b. Both employed and unemployed persons consume two different commodities,[6] a clean commodity to be denoted by c and a dirty commodity x. The consumer prices of the two goods are 1 and P, respectively. The consumer price of the dirty good includes a tax, so that $P = p + t$, where p is the producer price.

Firms hire labour at the wage $w(1 + s)$, where s is the rate of payroll tax. w is set by the trade union at a rate which exceeds the market clearing level. The resulting equilibrium in the labour market is illustrated by Figure 6.1. There is a fixed supply of workers, v, which will be identified with the number of members in the trade union. Given the wage rate, firms will maximize profits by hiring n workers; the number of unemployed therefore becomes $v - n$. The interesting question is now how the union's wage rate will be influenced by taxes, and in particular by a green tax reform which reduces the payroll tax and increases the tax on the dirty good.

All individuals, whether employed or unemployed, maximize utility subject to a budget constraint with a fixed income. Utility is $u(c, x)$, and the budget constraint requires that expenditure, $c + Px$ equals income, which in the case of the employed workers is

---

[5] Bean (1994) is a good survey both of the facts and of competing theoretical explanations of unemployment in Europe. For alternative—and complementary—analyses of the possible employment dividends of a green tax reform see e.g. Koskela et al. (1998), Bovenberg and van der Ploeg (1996) and Strand (1998).

[6] This is in contrast to Oswald's analysis, where workers consume only a single commodity and where relative prices accordingly play no role.

The Marginal Cost of Funds

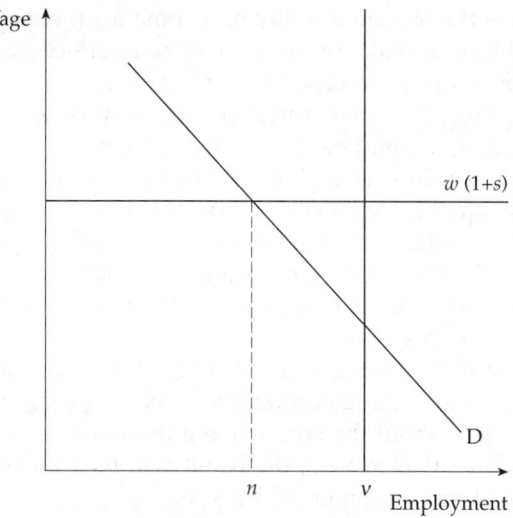

Fig. 6.1. Labour-market equilibrium with a monopoly union

w, and for the unemployed is b. The indirect utilities then become $v(w, P)$ and $v(b, P)$, respectively. The indirect utility functions are assumed to be strictly concave in income.

The union sets the wage rate that will maximize the sum of utilities of its members, taking into account that the number of workers employed, n, will be determined by the firms, once the wage rate has been set. Thus, the labour demand function is[7] $n = n(w(1 + s))$, with $n' < 0$. The union's preferences can accordingly be expressed by the utility function

$$U = n(w(1+s))\,v(w, P) + [v - n(w(1+s))]v(b, P). \quad (6.11)$$

The wage rate that maximizes union utility is then determined by the condition

$$\partial U/\partial w = n'(w(1+s))(1+s)[v(w, P) - v(b, P)] + n(w(1+s))v_w(w, P) = 0, \quad (6.12)$$

---

[7] In principle, the number of employed should also depend on the producer price of the dirty good, p. However, since this is assumed to be fixed, it does not appear explicitly in the function n.

where v_w is the marginal utility of income for the employed. For this condition to make sense, it must be assumed, as is natural, that $w > b$. Then the interpretation of the condition is as follows: by increasing the wage rate, the union pushes some of its members from employment into unemployment, and the utility loss from this is represented by the first term on the left-hand side of the last equality. Against this loss must be set the gain that the employed members of the union get increased incomes, and this is captured by the second term. At the optimum the marginal loss and gain must be equal to each other, and this is exactly what the condition requires.

Equation (6.12) determines the optimal w as a function of the payroll tax s and the environmental tax t. The presumption in policy debates about the employment dividend is that when s is lowered and t is increased, the result will be a lower wage rate (inclusive of the payroll tax). Firms will move down the demand curve for labour, employment will increase and unemployment will fall. Is this conclusion supported by the model?

Let D be the second-order derivative of the union's utility function; at the maximum we must have $D = \partial^2 U/\partial w^2 < 0$. Differentiating (6.12) with respect to s, we find that

$$\partial w/\partial s = (-1/D)[n''w(1+s)\Delta v + n'\Delta v + n'w v_w(w, P)], \qquad (6.13)$$

where $\Delta v = [v(w, P) - v(b, P)]$, is the utility gain from becoming employed. The sign of this derivative is that of the bracketed expression. Of the three terms, the last two are definitely negative. The first term is empirically likely to be non-negative, but less in numerical value than the last two terms. Then the whole expression is negative, implying that workers' wages increase when the payroll tax is reduced.

What counts for the employment decision, however, is not the wage rate w, but the labour cost faced by firms, which is $w(1+s)$. When a cut in s leads to an increase in w, it is not clear what happens to labour cost. Will it be true that

$$\partial(w(1+s))/\partial s = (\partial w/\partial s)(1+s) + w > 0?$$

Substituting in the expression from (6.13), we can rewrite the condition as

The Marginal Cost of Funds

$$n'(1+s)\Delta v + nv_w(\eta - \varepsilon) > 0. \tag{6.14}$$

Here $\eta = -v_{ww}w/v_w$ is the negative of the elasticity of the marginal utility of income, which is a positive number, while $\varepsilon = n'w(1+s)/n$ is the elasticity of demand for labour, which is negative. Applying the quadratic approximation

$$\Delta v = v_w(w-b) + (1/2)v_{ww}(w-b)^2,$$

some simple manipulations of (6.14) yield

$$\eta[1-(1/2)\varepsilon(w-b)^2/w^2] > \varepsilon(b/w). \tag{6.14'}$$

The expression in square brackets is positive, so this inequality always holds. The model therefore implies that when the payroll tax is reduced, the workers' income goes up, whereas labour cost goes down. This result is in fact qualitatively similar to the incidence effects of the payroll tax in the simple competitive model, although the analysis here is based on a different set of assumptions.

What about the second half of the green tax reform, the increase in environmental taxes? Recall that in the present model these taxes have no direct effects on the demand for labour, only on the union's wage claims, which in turn will influence firms' demand for labour. Intuitively, the increase in the price of dirty consumption goods will lead to a fall both in the real wage of the employed and in the purchasing power of the unemployment benefit. The first of these effects seems likely to lead to higher wage demands, while the second should lead in the opposite direction, since the standard of living for those who become unemployed will now be worse than before. To see whether the model lends some formal support to this intuition, we differentiate (6.12) with respect to t:

$$\partial w/\partial t = -(1/D)\{n'(1+\dot{s})[v_p(w,P) - v_p(b,P)] + nv_{wP}(w,P)\}. \tag{6.15}$$

At first glance, this expression does not seem to have any obvious economic interpretation. To simplify it we again employ an approximation, viz. $v_P(w,P) - v_P(b,P) = v_{wP}(w-b)$. We also use the fact that, by Roy's theorem, $v_{wP} = \partial(-v_w x)/\partial w$, and therefore

$$\partial(-v_w x)/\partial w = -v_{ww}x - v_w x_w.$$

Substituting into (6.15), we can rewrite this expression as

$$\partial w/\partial t = -(1/D)n(xv_w/w)[\varepsilon(1-b/w)+1][E-\eta], \quad (6.15')$$

where $E = x_w w/x$ is the income or Engel elasticity of demand for the dirty good. The sign of this derivative will be determined by the product of the two expressions in square brackets. Let us examine them in turn.

The first bracketed expression is the sum of a negative term and one. To guess at a reasonable value of ε, one would of course have to specify the type of employment, the length of the time period, etc. that one has in mind for a particular policy application. However, the estimates reported in Hamermesh (1986) seem definitely to indicate that for most applications it is realistic to assume that $-1 < \varepsilon < 0$. b/w is a number that can safely be assumed to be closer to one than to zero; in Norway it would be around two-thirds. But this means that the first bracketed term can be assumed to be positive, so that the sign of the derivative is determined by the second term in brackets.

An increase in the environmental tax is likely to raise wage demands if the income elasticity of the dirty good is high. This confirms our initial intuition; the higher the income elasticity, the more strongly will an increase in the tax reduce the standard of living of the employed, who have higher incomes than the unemployed. However, the tax increase is also likely to increase wage demands and unemployment if η is low. η is the elasticity of the marginal utility of income, and in this context this might be interpreted as the union's degree of *inequality aversion*.[8] In other words, the higher is the degree of inequality aversion, the less likely is the union to respond to an indirect tax increase by raising wages.

As we have seen, the theoretical prediction regarding the effect on wages and unemployment of an increase in green taxes is not very clear. In order to do a proper analysis of the effects of a tax reform, we should have to carry out a balanced budget tax inci-

---

[8] The elasticity will also be familiar to many readers as a measure of the degree of risk aversion. There is a close connection between the measures of risk and inequality aversion. The present model of trade union behaviour has indeed sometimes been formulated in terms of the choice of a wage rate to represent the preferences of a representative trade union member who perceives the risk of becoming unemployed as the actual unemployment rate, $(v-n)/v$.

The Marginal Cost of Funds

dence analysis, where there is a simultaneous reduction of s and an increase in t, so as to satisfy a constant revenue requirement, viz.

$$swn(w(1+s)) + t[nx(w, P) + (m-n)x(b, P)] = R. \qquad (6.16)$$

Given the complications involved in the partial analysis of tax changes, I shall not attempt to carry out such an analysis here, but it is clear that the conclusions regarding the final incidence on wages and unemployment will have to reflect the complications arising in the partial analysis of environmental taxes. A green tax reform is more likely to succeed in reducing unemployment (i) the lower is the income elasticity for dirty goods and (ii) the more egalitarian is the trade union in terms of its trade-off between the welfare of the employed and the unemployed.[9]

One aspect of the problem which has been neglected in the analysis is the direct influence of an improved environment on the union's wage demands. This assumption can be defended by assuming that utility is separable, so that there are no feedback effects on workers' demand behaviour, and that the union concentrates on promoting its members' 'material welfare', taking the state of the environment as given. From the point of view of descriptive realism, this is perhaps not a bad assumption. But one could also take a broader view, whereby the government tries to convince the union that a cleaner environment diminishes the need for high wages, thereby holding down the pressure for wage increases. In countries with strong unions, it is generally realized that major economic and social reforms are difficult to carry through without some kind of consent from them, and a major green tax reform would probably be no exception.

This is very much a partial analysis with a number of limitations. It takes as its point of departure a model offering a very specific explanation of the causes of unemployment, and it is obvious that a more realistic explanation would have to take a number of additional factors into account. It is also partial in the

---

[9] If the underlying utility function takes the Cobb–Douglas form $u(c, x) = c^\alpha x^{1-\alpha}$, it is easy to calculate that $E = \eta = 1$, so that the derivative (6.15′) becomes zero. The only element in the tax reform that counts in terms of employment is accordingly the reduction of the payroll tax, which, as we have seen, will always boost employment. But this case is a very special one, combining a unitary Engel elasticity with a unit value of the degree of inequality aversion.

sense of not claiming to take account of all economy-wide effects. Presumably the industry modelled here is only a part of the whole economy, and a full study of the effects of a green tax reform on unemployment would have to take account not only of the employment effects via the general wage level, but also of the effects which come from changes in relative wages, which will again lead to adjustments in the structure of industry. For example, if unions tend to be more egalitarian in dirty than in clean industries, a green tax reform of the type that I have modelled here is likely to be most successful in increasing employment in the industries that pollute most. This may perhaps suggest that one should have modest hopes for a single tax reform to result both in environmental and employment dividends. The thoughtful use of a number of different policy instruments will be required to reach such an ambitious goal.

6.4. Green Taxes and the MCF

The first clear statement of what is nowadays referred to as the marginal cost of public funds was provided by Pigou (1928; 1947: 34), who wrote:

> Where there is indirect damage, it ought to be added to the direct loss of satisfaction involved in the withdrawal of the marginal unit of resources by taxation, before this is balanced against the satisfaction yielded by the marginal expenditure.

In the context of the model of Section 6.2 this means that the direct resource cost per unit of public goods, p_z, should be increased by a factor which depends on the efficiency costs of the increased tax revenue needed to finance the additional expenditure; this is Pigou's 'indirect damage'. The nature of this factor was investigated in a famous article by Atkinson and Stern (1974), and since then it has been discussed by a number of writers.[10] In our context the question is whether greater reliance on environmental taxes will decrease the efficiency cost of the tax system and accordingly pave the way for increased public expenditure.

---

[10] See e.g. Browning (1987), Ballard and Fullerton (1992) and Håkonsen (1998).

Before turning to the analysis itself, there is one limitation of it that must be discussed in order to put the theory in proper perspective. Everyone agrees that the use of distortionary taxes imposes an efficiency cost on society. So why do we use them? The standard answer is that the use of the ideal individualized lump-sum taxes of welfare economics is impossible. But if we did not care about the distributive impact of taxes, we could levy uniform or arbitrary lump-sum taxes that would not create any tax wedges anywhere. The reason that this answer is unacceptable is that we also care about redistribution; accordingly, the main reason that taxes are distortive is that they are intended to be redistributional. Therefore, it becomes a little odd to argue that distortionary tax finance imposes a pure loss on the economy, since it presumably also leads to a distributional gain. This point was also realized by Pigou (1928; 1947: 32–3):

[A] government may properly engage in larger expenditures (1) the less even is the distribution of income among its citizens and (2) the more progressive is the revenue-raising scheme that it decides to employ.

Since the redistributional issue is not central to my main concern in this chapter, I shall ignore it in the formal analysis which follows, although the reader should keep the broader issue in mind. For further discussion of the interaction between redistribution and the marginal cost of funds the reader is referred to Wilson (1991), Dahlby (1998), and Sandmo (1998*a*).

Going back to the first quotation from Pigou, the indirect damage that he refers to is clearly what we would now describe as the efficiency loss from taxation. But if this is an argument for a marginal cost of funds in excess of one, one wonders if that argument also applies to green taxes, since these actually have positive effects on social efficiency. Could it possibly be the case that the MCF might be less than one when public expenditure is financed by green taxes?

In order to analyse this problem in more detail, it is useful to go back to the model of Section 6.2. In using it to study tax reform, we assumed that the supply of public goods was held constant. We now relax this assumption and look at the welfare effects of increasing the supply of public goods under alternative assumptions about the source of tax finance. With a variable supply of public goods the welfare differential (6.4) becomes

$$dW^* = dW/\lambda = I(-x_1 - mx_{21})dP_1 + I(-x_2 - mx_{22})dP_2 + (B - mIx_{2z})dz.$$
(6.17)

The last parenthesis represents the welfare effect of an increase in the supply of public goods. This consists of two terms. $B = Iv_z/\lambda$ is the social benefit in the Samuelson sense of the sum of the marginal rates of substitution between public and private goods. The second term is the additional environmental benefit that arises when an increase in the supply of the public good reduces the demand for the dirty good ($x_{2z} < 0$)—as when the construction of a public transportation system leads to less car use and a reduction of air pollution. However, if the dirty good were complementary in use with the public good ($x_{2z} > 0$)—e.g. with road construction leading to more air pollution from cars—there would be a negative environmental effect which should count as a deduction from the direct benefit of the public good.

Changes in taxes and public goods supply are restricted by the government's budget constraint (6.5). The differential of this is now

$$R_1 dt_1 + R_2 dt_2 + R_z dz = 0.$$

Writing this out in full, we obtain

$$I(x_1 + t_1 x_{11} + t_2 x_{21})dt_1 + I(x_2 + t_1 x_{12} + t_2 x_{22})dt_2 + I(t_1 x_{1z} + t_2 x_{2z})dz = p_z dz.$$
(6.18)

We may now study the welfare effects of increasing the supply of public goods under the alternative assumptions of 'clean' ($dt_1 > 0$, $dt_2 = 0$) and 'dirty' ($dt_1 = 0$, $dt_2 > 0$) finance. In the first case tax finance comes from higher taxes on commodity 1, in the second case by increasing the tax on commodity 2. Rather than studying the most general case I make the simplifying assumption that all cross-derivatives of the demand functions vanish, so that each demand function depends only on its own price. This is clearly much less than general, but the simplification still gives us a feel for the main considerations involved.

Take first the case of clean finance. With the assumptions that we have now made, the differential of the budget constraint becomes simply

$$I(x_1 + t_1 x_{11})dt_1 = p_z dz.$$
(6.19)

The Marginal Cost of Funds

Using this equation to substitute for dt_1 in (6.17) we obtain as a condition for an increase in the supply of public goods to be welfare improving[11]

$$B > (1+\theta_1\varepsilon_{11})^{-1}p_z = (\text{MCF})_1 p_z. \tag{6.20}$$

As before, θ_1 is the *ad valorem* tax rate and ε_{11} is the uncompensated price elasticity. With a downward-sloping demand curve the marginal cost of funds is indeed above one. If e.g. the tax rate is 20 per cent and the price elasticity is -1, the MCF for clean finance is 1.25.

Let us now do the same kind of exercise for dirty finance. We then set $dt_1 = 0$ and derive the condition for increased expenditure to improve welfare. Under the same set of simplifying assumptions this becomes

$$B > (1+m^*\varepsilon_{22})(1+\theta_2\varepsilon_{22})^{-1}p_z = (\text{MCF})_2 p_z. \tag{6.21}$$

Here $m^* = m/P_2$ is the environmental benefit as a percentage of the price of the dirty good. Comparing the two expressions for the MCF it is evident that in the case of dirty finance there is a modifying effect on the MCF through the environmental benefits of higher taxes. While a large price elasticity is bad from the conventional viewpoint of tax efficiency, it is good from the viewpoint of environmental efficiency. If the initial situation is one of uniform taxation and approximately equal price elasticities, it will indeed be the case that the MCF will be lower when public expenditure is financed by green taxes.

Will it also be true that $(\text{MCF})_2 < 1$? It is easy to see this will be the case if and only if $\theta_2 < m^*$. If this condition holds, the initial value of the tax rate is below the marginal social damage. This is in good accordance with the analysis of the optimal tax structure in the previous chapter. If the tax rate is below the level at which it exactly internalizes the environmental externality, there is a social benefit from increasing it, and tax finance is cheap in efficiency terms with the MCF being below one. If, on the other hand, it is above this level, then on the margin it is distortionary in the same way as taxes on clean goods, and the MCF is greater than one.

---

[11] In deriving the following condition I have assumed as before that an increase in the tax rate increases tax revenue, i.e. we are on the upward-sloping part of the Laffer curve.

In this analysis there is no presumption that the tax system satisfies the optimality conditions of Chapter 5. To discuss the MCF under such an assumption would be quite restrictive, especially since the MCF has now become a concept which is used in policy debates in many countries whose tax systems are unlikely to be optimal in the sense in which this concept has been used here. If the tax system had been optimal, it would clearly have been the case that the MCF would have been the same for clean and dirty goods; if the MCF were found to be lower for some forms of tax finance than for others, welfare could be increased by a tax reform, which is a contradiction of the optimality assumption. Whether the common value of the MCF would have been greater or less than one, depends on whether the level of spending on public goods is sufficiently small to be financed by environmental taxes alone. This is unlikely; even though it seems probable that the scope for using environmental taxes is much larger than indicated by their present importance, they are hardly likely to become the major source of government revenue in economies where the gross level of taxation is frequently close to 50 per cent of GNP.

As was the case in our discussion of the double dividend, the interpretation of the arguments surrounding the MCF depends crucially on the kind of thought experiment that one has in mind. Above I posed the question whether increased reliance on environmental taxes would decrease the efficiency cost of the tax system and pave the way for increased public expenditure. In the analytical model the question was formulated more precisely as whether, starting from some more or less arbitrary state of the tax system, the MCF is likely to be less for 'dirty' then for 'clean' tax finance. But the question could also have been formulated in a different way. Suppose that we start out with a system of taxes and public expenditure which has been optimized either without awareness of the scope for environmental improvement through selective taxes on dirty goods, or perhaps subject to the political constraint that commodity taxes should be uniform. Then the informational or political constraint is removed. The government now has in effect more instruments than before available for social-welfare maximization, so that potential welfare must go up. This conclusion follows from a basic mathematical insight. Suppose that you maximize a function of several variables subject to a constraint on some of the variables. Then the constraint is removed and the function is maximized again. The maximal value of the function must be higher in the latter case than in the former. The availability of green taxes has the potential to increase welfare. But does the increase in welfare also imply an increase in the public sector, as measured by expenditure on public goods?

Since the MCF is likely to fall as a result of using less distortionary taxes, one would perhaps expect the answer to this question to be an unqualified yes. But in fact it is not. Here we may draw on a result by Atkinson and Stern (1974), which established that although the MCF—a phrase coined later—is greater for distortionary than for lump-sum taxes, it does not necessarily follow that optimal public expenditure is lower in the former case. The present case presents a close analogy to this insight. More reliance on environmental taxes seems to move the optimal allocation of resources in the direction of the first best. But the first best does not necessarily involve more public expenditure.

If this sounds counter-intuitive, an example may be in order. In Chapter 2 we discussed a particular type of public good in the form of public expenditure on pollution abatement. The optimal level of expenditure on abatement must clearly depend on the amount of pollution generated by the private sector. But the use of environmental taxes will reduce pollution, hence the benefits of public abatement fall, and the use of resources on abatement should be reduced.

The marginal cost of public funds may be a useful tool for decentralized decision-making in the public sector. But it is a subtle measure which should be used with caution. It is a shadow price of resource use of the public sector, reflecting the efficiency of tax finance. But in a general equilibrium there is no simple connection between quantities and prices, and the informational content of this measure may easily be exaggerated.

7 Some Further Perspectives

7.1. Introduction

As a set of lectures this book is not meant to be an exhaustive treatment of the intersection between the two fields of environmental and public economics. Each of the fields is a major area of specialization, and even the intersection is such a large area that it would be hopeless to cover in any detail within a short book. In previous chapters I have therefore made a selection of topics which I either felt to be particularly central or where I had something specific to say. However, a selective treatment of a subject always involves a risk that one conveys a view of the subject as a whole that is not properly balanced. What is a balanced view is of course a matter of individual opinion, but my own attitude is that there are three topics which should at least be discussed briefly in order to put the treatment into proper perspective. The first is the international aspect of environmental problems, involving both international trade issues and problems of international policy coordination. The second is environmental pollution and its policy implications as seen from the point of view of the poor countries of the world. And the third is a further consideration of the political economy approach to environmental policy. In the following I accordingly present some brief reflections on each of these.

7.2. International Aspects of Environmental Policy

Does environmental policy need international coordination? An economist's natural response to this question would be that it depends on the precise nature of the environmental problem in question; in particular on whether there are international spillover effects of national pollution. Interestingly, however, in public debates about economic policy it has often been maintained that international coordination is needed in any case, because national policies are constrained by the need to preserve the country's international competitiveness. According to this view, if a polluting industry produces for the export market, national environmental policy should be designed in such a way that the competitive position of the industry with respect to its foreign competitors does not decline. A unilateral policy change is extremely unlikely to have this effect, so the conclusion is that corrective taxes or regulations should only be imposed if the environmental authorities in the foreign countries do the same; hence the need for coordination. The same argument would apply to a polluting industry which produces for the domestic market in competition with foreign producers. This general reasoning then seems to imply that in an open economy there is in fact little that can be done to improve the environment unless there exists an assurance that foreign competitors will be subject to the same policy measures.

To the economic theorist this analysis will hardly be convincing. Consider the analogy with the closed economy. Imagine that there are two industries, producing a clean and a dirty good respectively, where the pollution is associated with the production activity in the latter industry. The pollution affects only the area within the country's own jurisdiction. The government imposes a tax on the output or factor use in the dirty industry. The effect is that the dirty commodity becomes more expensive to consumers, demand falls and production is cut back. The sales revenue of the dirty industry is likely to fall, while that of the clean industry will increase. In other words, the dirty industry's market share will have fallen. This is unfortunate for the resource owners in the dirty industry, but it is a direct implication of what environmental policy is supposed to achieve.

Now consider the same problem in the context of an open economy which exports the dirty good. As environmental policy is enforced, e.g. by means of a green tax policy, the export industry contracts and the import-competing industry expands. There will be a new equilibrium, which, if the environmental policy is a sensible one, will have a better environment, a higher level of national welfare and a lower level of imports and exports, involving a smaller market share for the export industry and a higher market share for the import-competing industry. The logic of market adjustment to environmental policy is the same as in the closed economy case, and there is nothing in this line of reasoning that should lead one to attach a particular value to the reduction of exports. Note, incidentally, that the reduced competitiveness of the export industry has its counterpart in an increased degree of competitiveness for the import-competing industry.

There is of course nothing in the logic of environmental policy which should lead one to expect that it will necessarily lead to a reduction of exports; this is just a consequence of the way the example has been set up. If it had been the import-competing industry that generated the pollution, the consequence of a green tax reform would more likely have been to increase both imports and exports.

The example indicates that an open economy stands to gain from a green tax reform whether or not its trading partners adopt similar reforms; no international coordination is necessary. However, the conclusion should be interpreted with some caution. It particularly deserves to be emphasized that it is based on a comparative statics analysis which simply compares equilibria with no regard for the process of adjustment. Suppose that the country in question plans to introduce a green tax reform while its main trading partners do not. However, the government expects the governments of the trading partners to introduce similar reforms five years from now. These reforms are likely to have a significant effect on the world markets for the country's exports and imports. What should it do? If it goes on to introduce its own reform immediately, there will be a number of short-run effects from the readjustment process. If e.g. wages are sticky in the short run, there will be a period of frictional unemployment before the clean industry has been able to absorb the redundant workers. Then, once similar policies are adopted by the trading partners, there will be a new process of readjustment. If the domestic government decides on a wait-and-see policy, it may be able to circumvent a period of painful adjustment, but at the cost of a lower level of environmental quality for several years. Obviously, there is no general policy rule that can tell the government what the right course of action is. It will depend on the seriousness of the domestic environmental problem as well as on the magnitude of the adjustment costs.

Some Further Perspectives

However, even after the trading partners have adopted their green tax reforms, there is no reason to believe that the green taxes will be—or should be—the same in all countries. Even if all countries value the environment as a public good, this does not imply that they should all value it equally, nor that the cost of producing this public good—the cost of abatement—should be the same in all countries. After the adoption of environmental policies in all countries, some firms will therefore find that they are not as competitive as before. But if this is a reflection of a deliberate consideration of the costs and benefits of environmental improvement in each individual country, this should be seen as a necessary implication of those policies, not as an unintended consequence. It is not an argument for international coordination with the aim to equalize green taxes across countries.

Matters are different when we turn to externalities that cross national borders. Examples of this are numerous. Emissions into the ocean travel with the currents to pollute the coasts in other countries. Air pollution is carried with the wind to cause harmful effects to the natural environment far from the point of emission. There is solid scientific evidence for this which has also been utilized in the economics literature. A good example is Newbery's (1990) study of the acid rain problem. Acid rain stems from the emission of sulphur dioxide (SO_2) and nitrogen oxides (NO_x), which is caused by the burning of coal and oil. One effect of this is deteriorating air quality near the sites of emission. Other effects make themselves felt over long distances. Thus, acid rain is widely believed to have been the main cause behind the disappearance of fish from many rivers and lakes in the Scandinavian countries, and it was also considered to be a central factor behind the death of the forest, which has been a particularly strong concern in Germany. Acid rain is among those environmental problems that have become of less importance in recent years. Nevertheless, it will serve well as an example of transnational pollution.

The 1987 data for the origins and depositions of SO_2 in Europe, collected by the European Monitoring and Evaluation Programme and presented by Newbery (1990), demonstrate the transnational nature of pollution very clearly. To take one example, in 1987 the Scandinavian countries emitted 107 thousand tonnes per year (out of 16,695 thousand tonnes for Europe as a whole). Of this, they deposited 59 thousand tonnes on themselves, while receiving another 442 from other countries. The Scandinavian countries were therefore net receivers of this type of pollution; they received almost five times as much pollution as they generated. Great Britain, on the other hand, emitted 1,271 thousand tonnes, of which 700 were deposited on other countries, while total depositions in Great Britain were 702. Domestic depositions were accordingly about 55 per cent of emissions, making Britain a substantial net exporter. The overall picture is that while all countries both exported and imported sulphur pollution, an average of 50 per cent of their emissions got exported to other countries.

This picture adds another dimension to the discussion of incentives in environmental policy. In previous chapters we have focused on the incentives at an individual level and pointed out that a purpose of government policy in this area is to internalize the externalities that arise from uncoordinated individual actions. Here an additional problem of a similar kind arises at the government level. Suppose, for the sake of the argument, that every country had in fact adopted a policy that maximized the welfare of its citizens. Such a policy would, however, neglect the effects of the country's pollution on the welfare of other countries. From a global point of view, each country's policy would be based on an underestimate of the global damage caused by its own emissions. Uncoordinated country-specific policies would be insufficient to generate a global optimum, and there is a clear case for international coordination.

This conclusion presents a new challenge to the public economist. Starting from an international non-cooperative equilibrium of environmental policy, he would like to recommend that the world move to a cooperative equilibrium, where all externalities have been internalized. Two questions arise. First, how can such a cooperative equilibrium be characterized? Second, how can an international environmental policy be designed to sustain it?

To answer the first question, it is useful for a moment to look upon each country as an individual in the global economy.[1] We

[1] The use of words like 'global' and 'world' should not necessarily be interpreted literally. While some environmental problems are truly global, others may concern all countries in a region, e.g. the countries surrounding the North Sea. The general analysis here also applies to more limited groups of countries.

can then easily characterize the first-best solution by analogy with the analysis in Chapter 2. For each type of global pollution, abatement should be carried to the point where its global marginal benefit—equal to the sum of marginal benefits across countries—is equal to its marginal cost. If the global environmental problem is generated by a large number of countries, each with its national abatement cost function, an implication of this characterization is that the marginal cost of abatement should be the same in all countries. In other words, pollution should be reduced most in the countries in which emission reduction is cheap.

When it comes to implementation of this equilibrium, the analogy between the global community of countries and the national community of individuals runs into difficulties. In the latter case the payment of taxes and compliance with regulations is enforced by government authorities. In the former case there is no global authority which can levy taxes or impose regulations on firms and consumers in all countries. The implementation of a global environmental policy must be based on negotiations, and an agreement presupposes the voluntary participation by all countries involved. This is no simple matter, because, as illustrated by the case of SO_2, costs and benefits are likely to be very unequally distributed between countries. We now consider some methods which could be used in order to achieve a cost efficient allocation of pollution abatement between countries.

We first imagine that in the international negotiation it is proposed that pollution be regulated by means of a Pigouvian tax at a globally uniform rate, to be collected in each individual country. An internationally uniform tax—at a rate which reflects the aggregate marginal willingness to pay—would imply that the marginal cost of abatement would become the same in all countries, hence production efficiency would be achieved. Would such a proposal seem attractive to all countries? All countries would benefit from the improved global environment, but some much more than others. All would incur some costs, but some would have to pay a much larger share of the total costs than others. Countries with large benefits and small costs would be positive to the agreement, while those with small benefits and large costs would be against. There is the possibility that some of the countries in the latter group would reap a tax efficiency dividend from the reform, but this is hardly likely to be significant enough to secure universal agreement.

An alternative to this tax regime is one where the taxes collected nationally are paid to some international institution which has been set up by the countries for this purpose. The revenue is then distributed to the individual countries, not in the proportions in which they have been collected—that would have been pointless—but according to some agreed-upon sharing rule which secures that all countries gain by the agreement. Starting from the efficient allocation of emission cutbacks, the sharing rule would have to be designed in such a way that the countries with high benefits and low costs would transfer some of their surplus to those with high costs and low benefits. It is obviously essential for this type of agreement that there is simultaneous negotiation over the efficient distribution of cutbacks and the rules for sharing in the surplus. The general idea behind the scheme is to combine a policy of cost effectiveness with a system of fair division of the global surplus.

Yet another alternative regime for securing efficiency would be one with internationally tradable quotas. A global competitive market in quotas would result in a uniform price which profit-maximizing polluters would equate to the marginal cost of abatement; again, production efficiency would result. However, this regime must be based on some agreement concerning the initial ownership of the quotas. The distribution of ownership rights must form part of the bargaining in connection with the establishment of the quota system.

This brief sketch of alternative systems for international policy coordination clearly demonstrates the essential difference between global and national environmental policy. An international agreement on environmental taxes can secure efficiency, but runs into the problem that while some countries will be net gainers from the policy, other will be net losers. In the latter case, these countries will have poor incentives to participate in the agreement. An efficient tax scheme could conceivably be combined with a system of international transfers ensuring that all countries will gain, but bargaining over the distribution of the transfers will be difficult since some countries will in effect be required to pass some of their domestic tax revenue on to others. A market in quotas could also establish efficiency, but the initial distribution of the quotas raises problems similar to that of the distribution of tax revenues.

This distributional conflict is in some way reminiscent of that which emerges in the design of a national environmental policy. There too an efficient policy will normally involve both gainers (who benefit much from the environmental improvement but pay little in green taxes) and losers (who pay much of the taxes but get little in the way of benefits). The difference between the two cases, however, is very important. In a national setting the government can override the protests of the losers, given only that the gainers are in a sufficiently large majority. Moreover, a national government, at least in the industrialized countries, has a number of policy instruments that can be used to neutralize any adverse distributional effects of environmental policy. In the international community of countries, each country must participate in the agreement on a voluntary basis, which makes it important that every country gains from participation. This is particularly so since the scope for international redistribution is quite limited.

A number of researchers (Mäler, 1991; Chander and Tulkens, 1995) have in fact studied the design of international agreements that combine a regulatory scheme with a system for the distribution of the global gains between the participating countries so as to ensure that every country gains from participation. Numerical calculations such as those presented by Mäler indicate that the transfers involved between gainers and losers might be quite sizeable. Moreover, although a scheme of transfers may be constructed so as to satisfy the participation constraints for all countries, that still leaves considerable scope for the actual distribution of the net gains between them. Figure 7.1 illustrates the point.

Suppose that two countries, one rich and one poor, negotiate over the possible introduction of a global Pigouvian tax, the revenue from which is to be paid into an international environmental fund with a view to later distribution to the two countries. As the result of the treaty the net gain of each country will be its environmental benefit (in monetary terms) minus the amount of its tax payments. The magnitude of the calculated aggregate gains is shown by the position of the straight line GG' with a slope of minus one. The initial distribution of the gains is indicated by

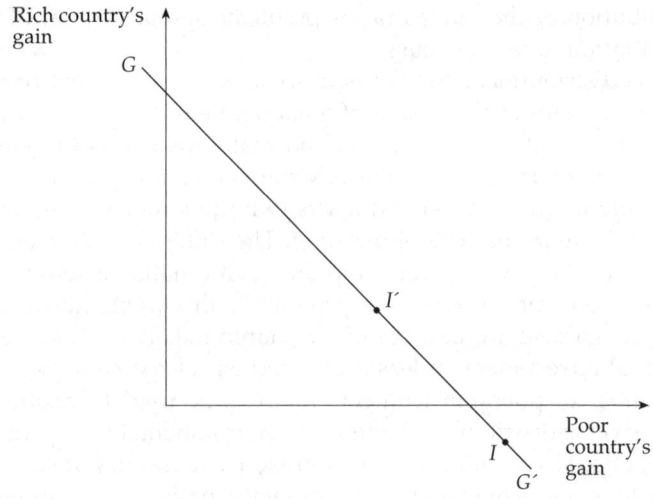

Fig. 7.1. The distribution of gains between countries

point I, which involves a large gain to the poor country and a loss to the rich country. This distribution could be explained by the assumption that the rich country is the main producer and exporter of the transnational pollution; the poor country, by contrast, produces little on its own but receives much of the pollution generated in the rich country. Given the position of the point I, the rich country suffers a net loss from the treaty, so that its participation constraint is not satisfied. To ensure its participation, the poor country must agree on a division of the tax revenue collected in the fund which moves the initial point I up along GG' to a position somewhere in the positive orthant, like I', where both participation constraints are satisfied. It is easy to see that this could possibly involve a payment to the rich country in excess of the amount of the poor country's tax payments, so that it would in effect make a money transfer to the rich.

But the position of point I' is so far quite arbitrary. If the participation constraints are interpreted to mean that any one of the two countries will accept a treaty that ensures a positive gain, then all points on GG' in the positive orthant will be possible outcomes of the negotiation, depending presumably on the negotiating skills and strengths of the two countries. Is this realistic?

Some Further Perspectives

Experiments with games seem to indicate that positive gains to both parties are not sufficient to ensure agreement to a treaty.[2] The parties will have some notions of fair division of the gains which must not be violated if agreement to the treaty is to be assured.

If the international treaty were based on a system of transferable quotas instead of a Pigouvian tax, the distributional problem would be that of assigning initial ownership to the quotas. This raises exactly the same problems about simultaneously ensuring participation as well as a distribution which is generally perceived as fair and just.

While notions of fairness may be important for the correct prediction of the outcome of the treaty, notions of justice and fairness are obviously also of importance if we imagine ourselves in the role of an outside arbitrator. Indeed, if we are to bring the parties to an agreement, it may be essential to make them adopt certain principles that would seem fair and just in a number of situations that are similar to this one, but where the initial allocation of gains are different. In the literature on transferable quotas, as summarized by Kverndokk (1995), it has been suggested the initial allocation of quotas should be made proportional to

- current emissions
- accumulated emissions
- real GDP
- land area
- population

To judge the merits and demerits of these criteria would take us too far afield here. But it must be emphasized that in a realistic view of the nature of international negotiations criteria of this kind must not be thought of as abstract principles of justice which can be imposed on countries from above. They must be criteria

---

[2] In the *ultimatum game* player 1 proposes a certain division of a sum of money, e.g. 100 kroner, to player 2. If player 2 accepts, that is the outcome of the game. If he rejects the proposal, none of them gets anything. On narrow assumptions about rationality, player 2 should accept any proposal (such as 99–1) that player 1 offers, provided only that player 2 receives a positive amount. But experiments show this prediction to be false. It turns out that player 1 will usually propose a division which is not far from an equal division and also that player 2 will in fact reject proposals which are too far from a 50–50 split. For a further discussion see e.g. Skyrms (1996: ch. 2).

of justice which the countries themselves will find acceptable as reasonable guidelines for their deliberations.

7.3. Environmental Policy in the Poor Countries

The analysis of the previous chapters has hardly made any explicit references to the development status of the country to which the analysis applies, nor has it been based on particular assumptions about its political institutions. However, it may be argued that most of the theory implicitly refers to a Western industrialized country. A central assumption is e.g. that most production takes place in firms, while households finance their consumption of market goods by income derived mainly from wage income. Another assumption concerns the nature of environmental pollution; the environment has been assumed to be in the nature of a public consumption good, affecting the welfare of consumers but not primarily the production potential of the economy. And a third assumption is that the government has at its disposal a wide range of instruments by which it can design policies so as to attain both environmental and other goals, such as an equitable distribution of income. None of these assumptions is especially attractive if the main goal of the analysis had been to study the problems of environmental policy in the poor countries of the world.

In many developing countries there is a large traditional sector which can best be described as subsistence agriculture, where families produce most of what they consume on their own (or communal) soil, mainly by means of their own labour. The most important effect that environmental pollution has on their lives comes through its consequences for the productive capacity of the natural environment or the *environmental resource base*, as Dasgupta (1996) calls it. In much of the environmental economics literature—as indeed in the present book—this aspect of environmental degradation has been neglected, the focus being instead on the environment as a public consumption good. There can be no objection to this as long as it is treated as an analytical simplification which must be adjusted and reinterpreted before being applied to concrete problems, which certainly involve both consumption and production issues in all types of economies.

Nevertheless, the analytical focus has probably tended to influence economists' perception of the major environmental issues in the developing countries. In the words of Dasgupta (1996: 390):

> [In] earlier days, environmentalists in Western industrial countries tended to focus on problems such as local air-pollution (e.g. sulphur emissions) and deterioration of amenities (e.g. national parks, beaches and coastlines). To the development economist, environmental matters, therefore, appeared a trifle precious, not wholly relevant to the urgencies of poor societies.

To many Western observers, this particular focus on environmental problems may also be responsible for the view that the benefits of environmental improvements are substantially lower in the poor countries because environmental amenities are 'luxury goods'.[3] But one's perception of this is likely to change once it is realized that environmental problems in the poor countries to a large extent mean a deterioration in the physical environment on which the standard of living of the rural population is based. Thus, environmental deterioration is a major cause of poverty. But, as Dasgupta and others have pointed out, there is also a reverse chain of causation whereby poverty causes environmental degradation. In times of severe hardship, such as are caused by severe droughts, floods or civil wars, the overriding objective of a poor family is to stay alive. If there is an urgent need for firewood, the result may be that the family cuts down the trees that in a longer perspective are of crucial importance for the prevention of erosion. There arises a dangerous dynamics in which environmental deterioration causes the environmental resource base to shrink, and where the resulting impoverishment leads to actions that cause further damage to the resource base.

Many observers have argued that these problems are made worse by the lack of well-defined property rights in many poor countries. Certainly problems like overgrazing of land and deforestation seem, from the property rights perspective of Coase (1960), to a large extent to be due to the distorted incentive structure that results from the prevalence of common ownership. This

---

[3] Some years ago this view was brought to the attention of the general public through the publicity received by a memorandum from the World Bank, in which it was suggested that industrial wastes should be exported to poor countries, where the evaluation of the environmental damage would be less than in the industrialized countries where the waste had been produced.

view of the connection between the nature of property rights and the overexploitation of the environment was made popular through the influential article by Hardin (1968) on the 'tragedy of the commons'.

The Coasian approach to the solution of the tragedy of the commons would be to establish property rights in the resource base so as to create better incentives for its long-run preservation. However, one should be careful about identifying such property rights exclusively with private property as usually conceived. It is tempting to conclude that in the absence of private property there is no one who takes an ownership interest in the common resource. But it has been well documented, notably in the work by Ostrom (1990), that there exists a variety of institutions for regulating the use of common property, so that the absence of private property rights does not automatically imply that the resource in question will be overexploited. When this happens, it may well be that the best reform is not privatization, but rather the development of better institutional forms for collective management.

We have previously seen that under first-best conditions, there is a strong case for designing environmental policies without any regard for their distributional consequences; any adverse effects on the distribution of income can be compensated by the adjustment of redistributional transfers. Even when we become more realistic in acknowledging that actual redistribution policy must rely on imperfect instruments such as progressive income taxes or social security, there is a more pragmatic case for the view that environmental policy in developed economies should primarily be considered in terms of efficiency. In developing economies the case for the pragmatic view is much weaker, simply because the scope for compensating redistribution policies is much less. On this background the discussion of the relative merits of alternative policy instruments, including that of improving the scope for collective action, may have to be reconsidered in the light of the institutional structure within which the instruments will be put to work.

There are other reasons why one should be cautious about recommending the adoption of environmental taxes and regulations in poor countries. One of the reasons (although not the only one) why poor countries do not have a redistributive tax system is that a progressive income tax is difficult to implement in a country with widespread illiteracy. But the same reason may also make it difficult to adopt some other forms of taxes or quotas. As an example, markets for transferable quotas are difficult to establish in a peasant economy, and any quota scheme needs a fairly sophisticated control system in order to make it function efficiently.

This having been said, one should certainly not conclude that the more standard approach to environmental problems is totally without relevance for the poor countries. First of all, the developing countries do have important sectors that are more similar to the industrialized countries than to their own sectors of subsistence agriculture. Furthermore, although a green tax reform may not be the most promising tool for environmental improvement,[4] the emphasis on the need to change private incentives so as to make it privately attractive to change one's pattern of production and consumption in a direction which leads to environmental improvement remains important and valuable. In fact, a number of development economists have used this general approach to suggest reforms that go primarily in the direction of changing the institutional framework of the economy. Institutions matter for the way in which market-based policies work. In the long run, institutional reforms and the development of market-based instruments for environmental improvement are not competing strategies for environmental development; they should instead be seen as being strongly complementary.

Many writers have seen the growth of population as the major threat both to economic development and to the preservation of the environment. It is clear that one can point to many cases where the pressure of population on the environmental resource base has apparently led to serious consequences, but it is not clear which policy conclusions should be drawn from this. If population growth itself is a source of negative externalities, should it be subject to a Pigouvian tax on children, as recommended e.g. by Harford (1998)? A serious objection to this view is the fact that

---

[4] The well-known book by Ahmad and Stern (1991) on tax reform in developing countries makes no reference to this or similar issues. But Dasgupta (1996) points to examples where the tax policy of a country actually encourages environmental degradation, so that a tax reform that did nothing more than establish neutrality would in itself have beneficial environmental effects.

to poor families children are not only a consumption good, but also to a large extent a factor of production; see Dasgupta (1993). A tax on children must therefore be expected to have extremely unfortunate distributional effects in many poor countries. But the incentives to bear children are strongly influenced by the social and economic structure. Structural reforms such as more provision of social security and better education for women offer a more promising strategy for achieving both a reduced pressure of population and a more humane and just society.

7.4. The Political Economy of Environmental Policy

Practically all of the analysis in this book has taken a normative approach to environmental policy. This is most obviously true of the chapters on taxation, where the objective was to characterize the set of taxes in the economy which would maximize social welfare. But it is equally true of the chapters dealing with benefit evaluation or alternative forms of environmental regulation, because there too the focus was on which procedures would best serve the maximization of social welfare.

It should be emphasized, however, that the analysis has been normative only in a conditional sense. No conclusion about desirable policies can be derived without assumptions about the objectives of the policy-maker, and in the analysis I have generally assumed that policy-makers are interested in policies that maximize social welfare or at least are consistent with some notion of social efficiency. Some people are very critical of this assumption. Welfare theorists are accused of being politically unrealistic or naïve in believing that politicians will actually implement the recommendations made by economists, because in reality politicians are moved by concerns which are entirely different from those of social welfare maximization.

These critics have an important point, but before taking it up in more detail, I would like to defend the welfare economics approach. First of all, I do not believe that politicians are unconcerned with efficiency or social welfare. It is indeed hard to believe that someone seeking political power in a democratic society should be totally unconcerned with the perceived welfare of the electorate, nor is it believable that he would be without

Some Further Perspectives

interest in ways to obtain more of some good without having to accept less of any other good. Nevertheless, one can easily see a number of reasons why politicians would not be prepared to follow all of the economist's advice or even accept the economist's suggested framework for thinking about a specific policy problem. They might have their own ideas and theories about the working of the economic system, or they might distrust the empirical findings of economic research. Moreover, they might have private incentives that are at least to some extent in conflict with the optimality criteria of welfare economics.

In spite of these reservations, I believe that there is an important role to play for normative economic analysis both in the design of environmental policy and of economic policy in general. Economic policy analysis does not fail if its analysis and recommendations are not immediately implemented by the political system; instead, its success should be measured by the extent to which it is seen as making a significant contribution to public policy debates. Economists must accept that their own contribution is only one among several, and that other recommendations may be in conflict with theirs.

These arguments notwithstanding, it is clear that there are other possible economic approaches to the study of the public economics of the environment. Instead of describing the social optimum we could ask which policy will in fact be chosen, given the objectives and constraints of the various agents in the policy-making game. This type of question gives an entirely different role to politicians and bureaucrats than the one implicit in the normative approach. Instead of being simply the recipients of economists' advice, they become agents in theories that aim to explain their behaviour, just as we attempt to explain the behaviour of consumers and firms in standard economic models.

While in normative theory one can with some justification speak of a standard set of models for the study of optimal tax and expenditure policies, this is not so in the area of positive political economy. Many approaches have been tried in different types of application; see the survey in Dixit (1996). One particularly influential contribution has been that of Grossman and Helpman (1994), who model the interaction between a government and several lobby groups in the determination of foreign trade policy. While a policy of free trade is efficient, deviations from free trade in the form of tariffs and subsidies may benefit particular interest groups (associated with the owners of sector-specific capital), and these are assumed to try to influence government policy by means of paying campaign contributions. These contributions are increasing functions of the degree of protection afforded by government policies. The government's objective function depends positively on these contributions, but also on the aggregate welfare of the consumers. By providing more protection for a particular industry, the government is able to collect a larger amount of contributions, but the inefficiency of protection harms consumer welfare. An optimal policy from the government's point of view must strike a balance between these two considerations.

The Grossman–Helpman framework is in principle applicable to a number of other areas of economic policy, including environmental policy. Just as in the case of foreign trade, it is natural to assume that the owners of 'dirty' industries are likely to be against attempts by the government to impose special taxes or regulations on them, and they will therefore be motivated to spend resources on attempts to make the government deviate from a policy of pure welfare maximization. But the disagreements about environmental policy are not simply a matter of a conflict between producer and consumer interests. As we have seen, there is no unambiguous relationship between individual welfare and the tax-inclusive price of the dirty good. From the point of view of private consumption, the effect on utility is negative. But if the tax succeeds in reducing the amount of environmental pollution, it makes a positive contribution to individual welfare. Whether, from an individual consumer's point of view, an environmental tax is a good thing, depends on the strength of his interest as a private consumer relative to his valuation of the environment as a public good, as well as on his perception of the effectiveness of tax policy. This was brought out in the analysis of the indirect utility function in Section 5.2. It may well be that some consumers in fact care very little about the environmental effect of the dirty good and are mainly concerned with their private consumption. Others may have no interest in the dirty good as a consumption commodity, but may on the other hand be much affected by its environmental aspect. Smoking is a good example of this. Smokers themselves are little affected by the environmental effects of smoking, and to them an increase in the price of tobacco implies an unambiguous welfare loss. Nonsmokers, on the other hand, find that their welfare is affected by the price of tobacco only to the extent that it succeeds in reducing smoking by others.

Although other examples may not be quite as clear-cut, there are a number of similar cases. Some owners of private cars take a strong delight in the consumption aspect of driving and feel that restrictions on car use entail a major loss of welfare. Others, including even some car owners, are so much affected by the externalities of car traffic that they would welcome such restrictions. So there are likely to be disagreements about environmental policy; moreover, because of the public good nature of the environment, disagreements are likely to persist even in situations where the design of environmental policy meets the criteria of Pareto optimality.

To convey the spirit of the Grossman–Helpman type of analysis, suppose that the government has an objective function, G, which has two components, campaign contributions, C, and consumer welfare, W. Assuming that welfare can be normalized to be expressed in units of the *numéraire*, the government's objective function can be written as a weighted sum of the two components, so that

$$G = C + \alpha W, \qquad (7.1)$$

where α is some positive number which expresses the weight that the government puts on consumer welfare relative to that on campaign contributions. Assuming that there are no other distortions in the economy, we may take consumer welfare to be a concave function of the tax on the dirty good, which we now write simply as t. Starting from $t = 0$, consumer welfare will first increase with an increase in t until it reaches a maximum at the optimal Pigouvian level of $t = t^*$. This is shown graphically as the bell-shaped curve $\alpha W(t)$ in Figure 7.2. t^* is the tax rate that would have been chosen under pure welfare maximization.

Since the campaign contributions come from producer interests that are harmed by the tax, these will be a decreasing function of the tax rate. This function expresses a menu of choice that the producer interests offer to the government. Starting from $t = t^*$, which is the highest conceivable value of t that the government will

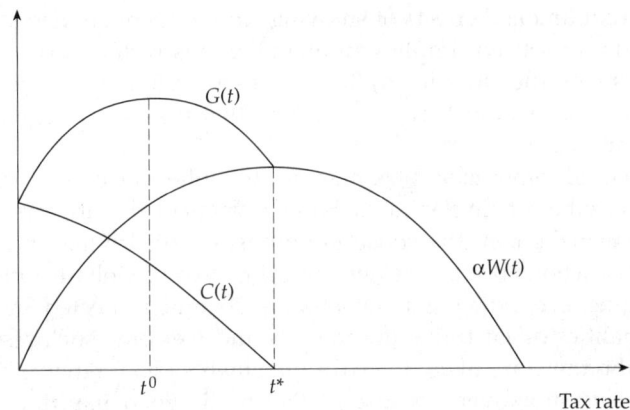

Fig. 7.2. The optimum and equilibrium values of the environmental tax

choose, contributions increase with a lowering of t, and it is natural to assume that they do so at a decreasing rate. The campaign contribution function can accordingly be shown as the downward-sloping curve $C(t)$ in Figure 7.2.

The government's objective function is now obtained as the vertical sum of these two curves and is shown as the curve $G(t)$. This has a maximum at $t = t^0$, which is necessarily lower than t^*. t^0 can be seen as the political equilibrium value of t and will represent a compromise between the government's concern for the welfare of consumers and the producer interests that provide funding[5] to increase the government's chances of staying in power.

In this analysis the only political pressure groups consist of organized producer interests whose purpose it is to restrain the environmental policies of a welfare-maximizing government. But to increase the realism of the analysis we have to take account of the fact that there are also lobby groups representing the interests of environmentalists who see it as their task to push the govern-

---

[5] In addition to direct funding in money terms, producer interests may assist the party in power in other ways, e.g. by helping to influence public opinion in favour of the government's policy both in the environmental field and in other areas. Such assistance too can be thought of as having a monetary value and therefore as being included in the function $C(t)$.

ment into adopting stricter environmental policies. The final outcome of the interaction between lobby groups and the political system will then be an equilibrium of conflicting forces, as analysed by Aidt (1998). It is interesting to note that both in the work of Grossman and Helpman and Aidt it turns out that the characterization of equilibrium environmental taxes includes elements of the Pigouvian tax principle. The conflicts over distribution modify this principle but do not discard it, simply because the government or the lobby groups also value efficiency. However, one could imagine other political disagreements over the principles of environmental policy that would result in equilibria where the contrast with efficient policies are more pronounced. It has often been observed that spokesmen for producer interests tend to prefer quantitative regulations and quotas over emission taxes, and one reason for this might be that quotas are likely to increase the barriers to entry for new firms, thus creating rents for the established firms in the industry.

This static analysis abstracts from the time dimension of the problem, which may be very important. In Chapter 2 we stressed the long-run nature of many environmental problems. The consumer welfare with which politicians should be concerned is therefore a present-value concept, expressing the value today of the environmental problems that are likely to prevail over a long future. Even if we assume that politicians are concerned with the welfare of consumers only for the reason of creating a feeling of goodwill towards themselves, this forces them to some extent to internalize the attitudes of the electorate. In trying to generate campaign contributions, however, the government must necessarily take a more short-sighted view, since the next election will in most cases be only a few years away. Thus, the influence from special producer interests may lead the government to a relative neglect of the more long-term aspects of environmental policy.

The geographical or regional dimension is also important for understanding the interaction between political and economic considerations.[6] The incidence of benefits and costs of environmental policies are often highly asymmetrical. In some cases the

[6] For an analysis that looks at the connection between immigration policy and transnational pollution in what can most naturally be interpreted as a political economy framework, see Sandmo and Wildasin (1999).

benefits may be local, while the costs of the policy are borne nationally. This will e.g. be the case when the government introduces stricter landing and take-off regulations at a big national airport. The people who reap the benefits are those living in the neighbourhood of the airport, while those who bear the costs are the transit passengers whose travels are delayed because of the regulations. Other cases will be characterized by national benefits but local costs. Policies that are introduced to preserve endangered animal species will benefit all nature-lovers in the country. But those who live in the same areas as the wild animals may have to bear the costs of wolves killing their sheep or deer grazing in their meadows.

Such asymmetries may have important political implications. A party in government that attempts to be re-elected to office will have to take account of what the various groups of producers and consumers see as the major issues in the election. Traffic delays because of landing regulations are unlikely to become a major issue; although they do inflict an inconvenience on a large number of people, the inconvenience to each of them is very small and is therefore hardly likely to be decisive for the way they vote. For the people who live in the neighbourhood of the airport, however, the noise from the planes leaving and arriving during the night may be extremely annoying, and the party that offers them the best protection from this is certain to get their vote. Vote-maximizing politicians will therefore have an incentive to emphasize the inconvenience to the neighbours of the airport much more, relative to the inconvenience to the travellers, than justified by a calculation of costs and benefits. In the case of wildlife preservation, the politicians' bias is likely to lie in the opposite direction. Those who benefit from the knowledge that wolves and moose roam the distant forests are still not very likely to let this issue dominate over the problems of unemployment and social security. But the farmers who count the losses in their herds of sheep or spruce tree plantations may feel very strongly that this impinges both on their employment and their security and will vote for the party that promises them to protect their economic interests.

It is not quite clear from this discussion whether, as a general rule, the political system in a democratic society can be said to be biased against environmental values. We have seen that one can make a case for the statement that politicians who are interested in re-election to office may be biased in favour of short-term benefits and in favour of policies where either the benefits or costs are concentrated among an identifiable group of voters. The examples indicate that this does not necessarily bias them against environmental policies. However, there is probably reason to believe that the solutions to some of the most important environmental problems involve benefits which are both very long term and with national or even global benefits, while at the same time requiring considerable costs in the short term to be borne by relatively small groups of consumers and firms. If this is the case, there is indeed some reason to worry about the ability of a democratic political system to handle environmental problems in a rational manner.

On this background one should perhaps not be surprised that some ardent environmentalists have come to adopt attitudes that are highly critical both to an economic system primarily based on the operation of market forces and to the democratic system of government. Their impatience with what they perceive as the wrong values and slow decision processes of the democratic system, coupled with their conviction that the solution to the environmental problems is a matter of great urgency, has led them to the view that more drastic measures are both necessary and morally justified.[7]

However, any criticism of the political and economic system which is currently prevalent in most Western countries should also consider whether the alternative is any better suited to achieve environmental goals. Although adherents of Soviet-style planning used to claim as one of its advantages that it was better able to handle the problems arising from the presence of externalities, the historical record of the communist countries shows

---

[7] The Norwegian king Olav Trygvason, who came to power in 995, had become a Christian during his foreign travels. When he came back to Norway, he started a process of forced conversion to his new faith, in part using very crude and brutal methods. One possible explanation of his behaviour was that, like many of his contemporaries, he was convinced that doomsday would come in the year 1000, at which time the heathens would be left to the fate of eternal damnation. This meant that he simply did not have time to convert people by the methods recommended by his religion, and if he ever had any doubts about his own procedures, he could always comfort himself by the thought that they were, after all, in the people's own interest.

something entirely different. From a theoretical point of view the claim was not unreasonable. After all, economists were fond of pointing out that environmental externalities could be diagnosed as cases of market failure. If the market system were abolished in favour of enlightened central planning, one might expect that its failures would vanish with it. There are obviously a number of reasons why this did not happen. One reason is that even a system of central planning must to some extent be departmentalized and decentralized, and the protagonists of socialist planning seriously underestimated the conflicts of interest that would arise in such a system, and which would prevent the attainment of a state where all externalities had been internalized. Another reason is evidently that the adoption of central planning went together with the abolishment of democratic political institutions (including independent legal institutions) and a free press. Environmental problems became official secrets, and those who were in a position to know about them did not dare to speak up.

There is a parallel here with the work of Sen (1981) on the analysis of the causes of hunger. Sen points out that there has never been a major hunger catastrophe in a democratic country, and he sees the main reason for that in the role of the press as a watchdog over inefficiencies and corruption. In a democratic society with freedom of expression, if people care about environmental deterioration, the press will pay attention to it and report on the development of environmental standards and on violations of environmental regulations. Another reason why the environment is likely to do better under democratic rule is clearly that politicians and public officials will be publicly confronted with incompetence or lack of action, partly through the attention of the media, partly through the activities of voluntary organizations in the environmental area.

Will the increasing importance of environmental issues lead to a greater role for public policy and central planning in market economies? It seems obvious that the answer must be yes, and it clearly requires new institutions for monitoring and regulation. But it is not obvious that a more active environmental policy inevitably leads to more public expenditure. First, much of the increased spending will have to be borne by the private sector which must use more resources to control the pollution resulting from its spending and consumption patterns. Second, although the public sector will have to increase its spending both on the environmental bureaucracy and on the improvement of public facilities, there are also offsetting effects. As an example, some of the adverse effects of environmental deterioration show up in the demand for health care, as when air pollution results in allergies and respiratory diseases. Air pollution also causes considerable damage to buildings (both private and public), and resources have to be used to keep them up. In both cases it is clear that a better environment will cause less demand for public spending, so that it is not clear what the net effect on public spending will be.

Although more emphasis on environmental problems does not necessarily involve more public expenditure, it does involve a more active role for public policy. It also involves economic planning of a rather sophisticated kind, since planners have to have a good understanding of the nature of market failure and of how the incentives of the market mechanism itself can be utilized to cure its own failures. Environmental policy is therefore a good example of a field where the failure of markets should not lead to a call for their abandonment in favour of the quantitative regulations of central planning. In a very large number of cases markets serve to allocate resources in a much more efficient way than could be achieved by central planning, and through appropriate intervention they can be made to work much better even in the cases where at present they perform poorly. A rational public policy must be based on an intelligent use of market incentives.

References

AHMAD, E., and STERN, N. (1991), *The Theory and Practice of Tax Reform in Developing Countries*. Cambridge: Cambridge University Press.

AIDT, T. S. (1998), 'Political internalization of economic externalities and environmental policy', *Journal of Public Economics*, 69: 1–16.

ALLINGHAM, M. G., and SANDMO, A. (1972), 'Income tax evasion: A theoretical analysis', *Journal of Public Economics*, 1: 323–38.

ARROW, K. J. (1951), 'An extension of the basic theorems of classical welfare economics', in J. Neyman (ed.), *Proceedings of the Second Berkeley Symposium on Mathematical Statistics and Probability*. Berkeley and Los Angeles: University of California Press: 507–32.

——(1953), 'Le rôle des valeurs boursières pour la répartition la meilleure des risques', *Econométrie*, 11: 41–7. English trans. as 'The role of securities in the optimal allocation of risk-bearing', in K. J. Arrow, *Essays in the Theory of Risk-Bearing*. Amsterdam: North-Holland (1974).

ATKINSON, A. B., and STERN, N. H. (1974), 'Pigou, taxation and public goods', *Review of Economic Studies*, 41: 119–28.

BALLARD, C. L., and FULLERTON, D. (1992), 'Distortionary taxes and the provision of public goods', *Journal of Economic Perspectives*, 6(3): 117–31.

BARRO, R. J. (1974), 'Are government bonds net wealth?', *Journal of Political Economy*, 82: 1095–117.

BAUMOL, W. J. (1971), *Environmental Protection, International Spillovers and Trade*. Stockholm: Almqvist & Wiksell.

——and OATES, W. E. (1971), 'The use of standards and prices for protection of the environment', *Swedish Journal of Economics*, 73: 42–54.

BEAN, C. R. (1994), 'European unemployment: A survey', *Journal of Economic Literature*, 32: 573–619.

BECKER, G. S. (1965), 'A theory of the allocation of time', *Economic Journal*, 75: 493–517.

——(1968), 'Crime and punishment: An economic approach', *Journal of Political Economy*, 76: 169–217.

BOHM, P. (1972), 'Estimating demand for public goods: An experiment', *European Economic Review*, 3: 111–30.

BOVENBERG, A. L., and DE MOOIJ, R. A. (1994), 'Environmental levies and distortionary taxation', *American Economic Review*, 84: 1085–9.

——and VAN DER PLOEG, F. (1994), 'Environmental policy, public finance and the labour market in a second-best world', *Journal of Public Economics*, 55: 349–90.

BOVENBERG, A. L., and VAN DER PLOEG, F. (1996), 'Optimal taxation, public goods and environmental policy with involuntary unemployment', *Journal of Public Economics*, 62: 59–83.

BROWNING, E. K. (1987), 'On the marginal welfare cost of taxation', *American Economic Review*, 77: 11–23.

BUCHANAN, J. M. (1969), 'External diseconomies, corrective taxes, and market structure', *American Economic Review*, 59: 174–6.

CHANDER, P., and TULKENS, H. (1995), 'A core-theoretic solution for the design of cooperative agreements on transfrontier pollution', *International Tax and Public Finance*, 2: 279–93.

CHRISTIANSEN, V. (1981), 'Evaluation of public projects under optimal taxation', *Review of Economic Studies*, 48: 447–57.

CLARKE, E. H. (1971), 'Multipart pricing of public goods', *Public Choice*, 11: 17–33.

COASE, R. H. (1960), 'The problem of social cost', *Journal of Law and Economics*, 3: 1–44.

CORLETT, W. J., and HAGUE, D. C. (1953–4), 'Complementarity and the excess burden of taxation', *Review of Economic Studies*, 21: 21–30.

CORNES, R. (1980), 'External effects: An alternative formulation', *European Economic Review*, 14: 307–21.

COWELL, F. A. (1990), *Cheating the Government. The Economics of Tax Evasion*. Cambridge, Mass.: MIT Press.

CROPPER, M. L., and OATES, W. E. (1992), 'Environmental economics: A survey', *Journal of Economic Literature*, 30: 675–740.

DAHLBY, B. (1998), 'Progressive taxation and the social marginal cost of public funds', *Journal of Public Economics*, 67: 105–22.

DASGUPTA, P. (1993), 'Poverty, resources and fertility: the household as a reproductive partnership', in A. B. Atkinson (ed.), *Alternatives to Capitalism*. London: Macmillan, in association with the International Economic Association: 207–43.

——(1996), 'The economics of the environment', *Environment and Development Economics*, 1: 387–428.

DEBREU, G. (1959), *Theory of Value*. New York: Wiley.

DIAMOND, P. A. (1973), 'Consumption externalities and imperfect corrective pricing', *Bell Journal of Economics and Management Science*, 4: 526–38.

——and HAUSMANN, J. A. (1994), 'Contingent valuation: Is some number better than no number?', *Journal of Economic Perspectives*, 8(4): 45–64.

——and MIRRLEES, J. A. (1971), 'Optimal taxation and public production I–II', *American Economic Review*, 61: 8–27 and 261–78.

————(1973), 'Aggregate production with consumption externalities', *Quarterly Journal of Economics*, 87: 1–24.

DIXIT, A. K. (1975), 'Welfare effects of tax and price changes', *Journal of Public Economics*, 4: 103–23.

—— (1996), *The Making of Economic Policy: A Transaction-Cost Politics Perspective*. Cambridge, Mass.: MIT Press.

—— and PINDYCK, R. S. (1994), *Investment under Uncertainty*. Princeton, NJ: Princeton University Press.

DRÈZE, J., and STERN, N. (1987), 'The theory of cost-benefit analysis', ch. 14 in A. J. Auerbach and M. Feldstein (eds.), *Handbook of Public Economics*, ii. Amsterdam: North-Holland.

FELDSTEIN, M. (1976), 'On the theory of tax reform', *Journal of Public Economics*, 6: 77–104.

FREY, B. S. (1997), 'A constitution for knaves crowds out civic virtues', *Economic Journal*, 107: 1043–53.

—— OBERHOLZER-GEE, F., and EICHENBERGER, R. (1996), 'The old lady visits your backyard: A tale of morals and markets', *Journal of Political Economy*, 104: 1297–313.

FULLERTON, D. (1997), 'Environmental levies and distortionary taxation: Comment', *American Economic Review*, 87: 245–51.

GOULDER, L. H. (1995), 'Environmental taxation and the double dividend: A reader's guide', *International Tax and Public Finance*, 2: 157–83.

GROSSMAN, G. M., and HELPMAN, E. (1994), 'Protection for sale', *American Economic Review*, 84: 833–50.

GROVES, T., and LEDYARD, J. O. (1977), 'Optimal allocation of public goods: A solution to the free rider problem', *Econometrica*, 45: 783–809.

HAHN, F. H. (1973), 'On optimum taxation', *Journal of Economic Theory*, 6: 96–106.

HÅKONSEN, L. (1998), 'An investigation into alternative representations of the marginal cost of public funds', *International Tax and Public Finance*, 5: 329–43.

HAMERMESH, D. S. (1986), 'The demand for labor in the long run', ch. 8 in O. Ashenfelter and R. Layard (eds.), *Handbook of Labor Economics*, i. Amsterdam: North-Holland.

HANEMANN, W. M. (1994), 'Valuing the environment through contingent valuation', *Journal of Economic Perspectives*, 8(4): 19–43.

HARBERGER, A. C. (1971), 'Three basic postulates for applied welfare economics: An interpretive essay', *Journal of Economic Literature*, 9: 785–97.

HARDIN, G. (1968), 'The tragedy of the commons', *Science*, 162: 1243–8.

HARFORD, J. D. (1978), 'Firm behavior under imperfectly enforceable pollution standards and taxes', *Journal of Environmental Economics and Management*, 5: 26–43.

—— (1987), 'Self-reporting of pollution and the firm's behavior under imperfectly enforceable regulations', *Journal of Environmental Economics and Management*, 14: 293–303.

—— (1998), 'The ultimate externality', *American Economic Review*, 88: 260–5.

HOLLÄNDER, H. (1990), 'A social exchange approach to voluntary cooperation', *American Economic Review*, 80: 1157–67.
IRELAND, N. J. (1977), 'Ideal prices vs. prices vs. quantities', *Review of Economic Studies*, 44: 183–6.
JOHANSEN, L. (1965), *Public Economics*. Amsterdam: North-Holland.
—— (1977a), 'The theory of public goods: Misplaced emphasis?', *Journal of Public Economics*, 7: 147–52.
—— (1977b), 'Eierforhold og styringsmuligheter', *Sosialøkonomen*, 31(2): 10–16; repr. in L. Johansen, *Kriser og beslutningssystemer i samfunnsøkonomien*. Oslo: Universitetsforlaget, 1983.
KOSKELA, E., SCHÖB, R., and SINN, H.-W. (1998), 'Pollution, factor taxation and unemployment', *International Tax and Public Finance*, 5: 379–96.
KVERNDOKK, S. (1995), 'Tradeable CO_2 emission permits: Initial distribution as a justice problem', *Environmental Values*, 4: 129–48.
KWEREL, E. (1977), 'To tell the truth: Imperfect information and optimal pollution control', *Review of Economic Studies*, 44: 595–601.
LANCASTER, K. J. (1966), 'A new approach to consumer theory', *Journal of Political Economy*, 74: 132–57.
LINDAHL, E. (1919), *Die Gerechtigkeit der Besteuerung*. Lund: Gleerup.
LIPSEY, R. G., and LANCASTER, K. (1956–7), 'The general theory of second best', *Review of Economic Studies*, 24: 11–32.
MÄLER, K.-G. (1991), 'Environmental issues in the new Europe', in A. B. Atkinson and R. Brunetta (eds.), *Economics for the New Europe*. London: Macmillan, in association with the International Economic Association: 262–87.
MARRELLI, M. (1984), 'On indirect tax evasion', *Journal of Public Economics*, 25: 181–96.
MEADE, J. E. (1952), 'External economies and diseconomies in a competitive situation', *Economic Journal*, 62: 54–67.
—— (1973), *The Theory of Economic Externalities*. Leiden: A. W. Sijthoff.
MIRRLEES, J. A. (1971), 'An exploration in the theory of optimum income taxation', *Review of Economic Studies*, 38: 175–208.
MUSGRAVE, R. A. (1959), *The Theory of Public Finance*. New York: McGraw-Hill.
MUTH, R. F. (1966), 'Household production and consumer demand functions', *Econometrica*, 34: 699–708.
NEWBERY, D. M. G. (1990), 'Acid rain', *Economic Policy*, 11: 297–346.
OKUN, A. M. (1975), *Equality and Efficiency: The Big Tradeoff*. Washington, DC: Brookings Institution.
OSTROM, E. (1990), *Governing the Commons: The Evolution of Institutions for Collective Action*. Cambridge: Cambridge University Press.
OSWALD, A. J. (1985), 'The economic theory of trade unions: An introductory survey', *Scandinavian Journal of Economics*, 87: 160–93.
PALMER, K., OATES, W. E., and PORTNEY, P. R. (1995), 'Tightening envi-

ronmental standards: The benefit-cost or the no-cost paradigm?', *Journal of Economic Perspectives*, 9(4): 119–32.
PIGOU, A. C. (1912), *Wealth and Welfare*. London: Macmillan
——(1920), *The Economics of Welfare*, 4th edn. 1932. London: Macmillan.
——(1928), *A Study in Public Finance*, 3rd edn, 1947. London: Macmillan.
PORTER, M. E., and VAN DER LINDE, C. (1995), 'Toward a new conception of the environment–competitiveness relationship', *Journal of Economic Perspectives*, 9(4): 97–118.
PORTNEY, P. R. (1994), 'The contingent valuation debate: Why economists should care', *Journal of Economic Perspectives*, 8(4): 3–17.
RAMSEY, F. P. (1927), 'A contribution to the theory of taxation', *Economic Journal*, 37: 47–61.
——(1928), 'A mathematical theory of saving', *Economic Journal*, 38: 543–59.
SAMUELSON, P. A. (1954), 'The pure theory of public expenditure', *Review of Economics and Statistics*, 36: 387–9.
——(1958), *Economics. An Introductory Analysis*, 4th edn. New York: McGraw-Hill.
SANDMO, A. (1973), 'Public goods and the technology of consumption', *Review of Economic Studies*, 40: 517–28.
——(1975), 'Optimal taxation in the presence of externalities', *Swedish Journal of Economics*, 77: 86–98.
——(1976a), 'Direct versus indirect Pigovian taxation', *European Economic Review*, 7: 337–49.
——(1976b), 'Optimal taxation: An introduction to the literature', *Journal of Public Economics*, 6: 37–54.
——(1980), 'Anomaly and stability in the theory of externalities', *Quarterly Journal of Economics*, 94: 799–807.
——(1983), 'Ex post welfare economics and the theory of merit goods', *Economica*, 50: 19–33.
——(1987), 'A reinterpretation of elasticity formulae in optimum tax theory', *Economica*, 54: 89–96.
——(1993), 'Optimal redistribution when tastes differ', *Finanzarchiv*, 50: 149–63.
——(1998a), 'Redistribution and the marginal cost of public funds', *Journal of Public Economics*, 70: 365–82.
——(1998b), 'Efficient environmental policy with imperfect compliance', Discussion Paper 8/98, Department of Economics, Norwegian School of Economics and Business Administration.
——and WILDASIN, D. E. (1999), 'Taxation, migration and pollution', *International Tax and Public Finance*, 6: 39–59.
SAVAGE, L. J. (1954), *The Foundations of Statistics*. New York: Wiley.
SEN, A. K. (1981), *Poverty and Famines: An Essay on Entitlement and Deprivation*. Oxford: Clarendon Press.

SIEBERT, H. (1995), *Economics of the Environment*, 4th edn. Berlin-Heidelberg: Springer.

SINN, H.-W. (1993), 'Pigou and Clarke join hands', *Public Choice*, 75: 79–91.

SKYRMS, B. (1996), *Evolution of the Social Contract*. Cambridge: Cambridge University Press.

SMITH, A. (1776), *An Inquiry into the Nature and Causes of the Wealth of Nations*. Edinburgh.

SRINIVASAN, T. N. (1973), 'Tax evasion: A model', *Journal of Public Economics*, 2: 339–46.

STIGLER, G. J., and BECKER, G. S. (1977), 'De gustibus non est disputandum', *American Economic Review*, 67: 76–90.

STRAND, J. (1998), 'Pollution taxation and revenue recycling under monopoly unions', *Scandinavian Journal of Economics*, 100: 765–80.

SUCHANEK, G. L. (1979), 'Information, optimality and pollution control', *Journal of Public Economics*, 12: 99–114.

VICKREY, W. (1961), 'Counterspeculation, auctions and competitive sealed tenders', *Journal of Finance*, 16: 8–37.

WEITZMAN, M. L. (1974), 'Prices vs. quantities', *Review of Economic Studies*, 41: 477–91.

WILSON, J. (1991), 'Optimal public good provision with limited lump-sum taxation', *American Economic Review*, 81: 153–66.

Index

acid rain 27, 74, 133
additivity property (of taxes) 101, 106
administrative costs 25, 91, 108
agriculture 1, 3, 140, 143
Ahmad, E. 143
Aidt, T. S. 149
air pollution 1, 5, 6, 8, 17, 73, 76, 107, 126, 133, 153
Allingham, M. G. 57
altruism 38
Arrow, K. J. 35, 40, 41, 53
Atkinson, A. B. 124, 129
auction 16, 45, 64, 79

Ballard, C. L. 124
Barro, R. J. 38
Baumol, W. J. 26, 49
Bean, C. R. 118
Becker, G. S. 57, 65, 72
biodiversity 3
Bohm, P. 70
Bovenberg, A. L. 101, 118
Browning, E. K. 124
Buchanan, J. M. 14

campaign contributions 146, 147, 149
central planning 2, 3, 152, 153
Chander, P. 137
Christiansen, V. 86
Clarke, E. H. 80, 84
Clarke tax 80, 81, 83
climate gases 22, 43
Coase, R. H. 26, 141
common property 142
competitiveness 21, 67, 131, 132
compliance 16, 17, 63, 67, 135
congestion 1, 6, 8, 10, 28, 47, 72, 76, 93, 94
contingent valuation 76–9, 84–5
Corlett, W. J. 115
Cornes, R. 93
Cowell, F. A. 59
Cropper, M. L. 26, 70, 73, 74

Dahlby, B. 125
Dasgupta, P. 140, 141, 143, 144
deadweight loss 10
Debreu, G. 35, 40, 41, 53
demand-revealing mechanism 79–85
Diamond, P. A. 32, 46, 76, 78, 91, 106
discounting 36–40, 43
distributional characteristic 103–4, 108
distributional justice 5, 30, 44
distributional weights 87–8
Dixit, A. K. 43, 116, 145
double dividend 12, 26, 109–24, 128
Drèze, J. 88
dynamic models 37

energy 15
environmental damage function 28, 31, 34–41, 82, 92, 111
environmental feedback 93, 98–9, 111
environmental resource base 140–3
equity 2
expected utility 41, 59, 62

Feldstein, M. 111
free good 3
Frey, B. S. 67, 89
Fullerton, D. 101, 124
future generations 19, 23, 38

global commons 22
global warming 1, 22, 66, 107
Goulder, L. H. 26, 113
grandfathering of quotas 24, 65
Grossman, G. M. 145–9
Groves, T. 80, 84

Hague, D. C. 115
Hahn, F. H. 102
Håkonsen, L. 124
Hamermesh, D. S. 122
Hanemann, W. M. 76, 78
Harberger, A. C. 86–8
Hardin, G. 26, 142
Harford, J. D. 60, 63, 143

Hausmann, J. A. 76, 78
hedonic price approach 74
Helpman, E. 145–9
Holländer, H. 67
household production 72–6, 85, 106
housing 34, 74–5

inequality 20, 103, 108
inequality aversion 122–3
international agreements 21–2, 136–7
international coordination 130–1, 132, 133, 134
invisible hand, 4–5, 9
Ireland, N. J. 53

Johansen, L. 25, 70, 87

Koskela, E. 118
Kverndokk, S. 139
Kwerel, E. 80

Laffer curve 100, 114, 127
Lancaster, K. J. 72, 90
Ledyard, J. O. 80, 84
Lindahl, E. 33
Lindahl taxation 33
Linde, C. van der 67
Lipsey, R. G. 90
lobby groups 14, 145, 148, 149

Mäler, K.-G. 137
marginal cost of public funds 124–9
market failure 4, 9–10, 19, 44, 90, 101, 152, 153
Marrelli, M. 59
Meade, J. E. 25, 26
Mirrlees, J. A. 46, 91, 102
mixed economy 4
monitoring of emissions 14, 57–63, 106, 152
monopoly 13–14, 20
monopoly union model 117
Mooij, R. A. de 101
Musgrave, R. A. 25
Muth, R. F. 72

Newbery, D. M. G. 133

Oates, W. E. 26, 49, 70, 73, 74
Okun, A. M. 20
option value 19, 43
Ostrom, E. 142
Oswald, A. J. 118

Palmer, K. 67
Pareto optimum 5, 31
persuasion 45, 65–7
Pigou, A. C. 8, 18, 73, 105, 124, 125
Pigouvian taxes:
 in first-best situations 32–42
 and marginal cost of public funds 124–9
 partial equilibrium analysis 8–15
 in second best situations 90–108
 versus regulations 45–65
Pindyck, R. S. 43
Ploeg, F. van der 118
political economy 22–4, 130, 144–53
poor countries 130, 140–4
population 139, 143–4
Porter, M. E. 67
Portney, P. R. 76, 77
poverty 141
present value 18, 39, 64, 149
pressure groups 23, 148
prisoners' dilemma 6
private and social marginal benefit 10–12
private and social marginal cost 8–10, 12–14
property rights 16, 26, 141–2

quotas 15–17, 24
 and barriers to entry 149
 international distribution of 136–7, 139
 in poor countries 143
 versus taxes 45–65

Ramsey, F. P. 39, 91, 98–100, 104, 114
redistribution 5, 19–20, 33, 87–8, 102–5, 115, 125, 137, 142
revelation of preferences 33, 69–70, 70–85
revenue recycling 110
rights perspective 89
risk aversion 59, 62–3, 122
risk neutrality 62–3

Samuelson, P. A. 2, 27, 29–30, 33, 44, 69, 126
Sandmo, A. 46, 57, 63, 72, 91, 93, 98, 99, 101, 102, 106, 115, 125, 149
Savage, L. J. 41
Sen, A. K. 152
Siebert, H. 37
Sinn, H.-W. 80

Index

Skyrms, B. 139
Smith, A. 4–5
social security 20, 105, 142, 144, 150
social welfare function 29, 41, 91, 95, 103, 108, 111
spillover effect 21, 89, 130
Srinivasan, T. N. 57
Stern, N. 88, 124, 129, 143
Stigler, G. J. 65
Strand, J. 118
Suchanek, G. L. 80
survey research 78

targeting 100, 106
tax evasion 57–63
tradable quotas 63–5

transnational pollution 89, 133, 138, 149
Tulkens, H. 137

ultimatum game 139
unemployment 105, 110, 117–24, 132, 150

Vickrey, W. 79
voluntary agreements 65–7

water pollution 16, 66, 72, 93–4, 105
Weitzman, M. L. 53–7
Wildasin, D. E. 149
Wilson, J. 125